THE SILENT WEAPONS

Also by Robin Clarke

THE DIVERSITY OF MAN

THE
SILENT WEAPONS

by Robin Clarke

DAVID McKAY COMPANY, INC.

NEW YORK

THE SILENT WEAPONS

COPYRIGHT © 1968 BY ROBIN CLARKE

LIBRARY OF CONGRESS CATALOG CARD NUMBER: 68-18469

MANUFACTURED IN THE UNITED STATES OF AMERICA

To my colleagues at *Science Journal*, who for a year patiently withstood interminable discussions about toxic weapons while this book was being written

ACKNOWLEDGMENTS

A BOOK OF THIS KIND never has a single author. In this case, most of the facts have been provided, or ferreted out, by other people. My job has been to assemble them. Most of the facts have also appeared previously in print, though often in somewhat obscure hiding places. Nor can I claim any great originality for the ideas in the book, many of which have been previously printed and only a few of which are my own. I therefore owe a debt of gratitude to the many scientists, officials, and laymen who have provided both figures and concepts and have allowed me to use them secondhand. Many of these people would have no objection to their names being mentioned, but others have specifically asked for this not to be done. Under the circumstances, it seems better to thank them, and those who read the book for technical accuracy, anonymously.

Contents

Introduction

THE GLORY OF WAR is said to have finally disappeared in the mud of Flanders. Since then, science and technology have so changed military thought that even the function of war has become clouded in obscurity. But together with these technical changes has come a profound reversal of attitude toward the morality of conflict and the rules by which it should be waged.

It was during the First World War that strategists began to evaluate the civilian population as an important military target. Although the proportion of civilians killed in that war was small, it increased to huge proportions in World War II. With the German blitzkrieg, and the Allies' bombing technique of turning German cities into fireballs, there came a new philosophy of war, which hinged on both the importance of the civilian target and its vulnerability. By the end of the war, it seemed, this trend had reached its illogical conclusion. The invention of nuclear weapons had made it possible for a handful of men in a flight of aircraft to obliterate the civilian target from the face of a continent.

Today, the nuclear weapon remains our most immediate threat. But it is not the end point of the military trend which has been called the "escalation of brutality." A further development, for the most part lying behind the security barriers of the major powers, has already loomed over the horizon—the chemical and biological weapons that are the subject of this book.

The chemical weapons have, of course, already been used on a large scale in World War I. So it may seem as though the threat they represent is neither novel nor severe. Nothing could be further from the truth. These now obsolete chemicals bear a similar relationship to modern toxic weapons as the first atomic pile, which Enrico Fermi built in a squash court in Chicago, did to the hydrogen bomb. The new toxic weapons have never been used in war; their capabilities remain unknown to most military personnel and to nearly all civilians. Not only are they truly novel weapons, but they represent a threat to civilians exceeded only by nuclear weapons.

In a sense, too, they pose a novel moral problem. World War I propaganda stirred nations into a frenzy of indignation when gas warfare was first used in France in 1915. Yet there was nothing intrinsically more inhumane or more barbaric about the World War I chemical weapons than there was about the use of high-explosive shells. In fact, the chemicals proved a good deal more effective than other weapons, produced a lower proportion of deaths to injuries, and are generally thought to have given rise to less intense suffering and fewer long-lived aftereffects than almost any other kind of weapon. But it is not on this plane that toxic weapons have now become morally repugnant.

The biological weapons being developed today are unique in at least one respect. They are the only weapons that have ever been invented for the single purpose of annihilating civilian populations. Even nuclear weapons, which certainly could produce a similar devastation, find other uses—in war for knocking out military and industrial sites, and in peace for deepening harbors, excavating ditches and tunnels, and revealing details of the earth's structure. Biological weapons are uniquely anticivilian devices. In war they might find limited use against troops, as well, but they could never be used to attack or destroy sites or buildings. In peace, they have no applications of any kind.

The biological weapons pose other problems that to some people appear even more severe. For obvious reasons, these weapons cannot be tested before use in the sense that other weapons can. This means that when—or if—they ever are used in war, they will achieve a notorious military first: they will be the first weapons of any scale to have been liberated on an enemy before the range of possible effects of those weapons was known with accuracy. Even more appalling, this first use of a biological weapon will in reality also be its first full-scale test; as such, it will constitute a human experiment of a magnitude far outstripping even those that were perpetrated in the Nazi prison camps.

Biological weapons also threaten the ecology of our planet —or at least a substantial portion of it—to a greater extent than even nuclear weapons do. There is a chance that if a large-scale nuclear attack is launched, it could produce a permanent change in the balance of nature. But this would be a secondary effect, for the prime purpose of the attack would be to destroy property and people. It would have only a side effect, so to speak, on animal and plant life, killing off some species and leaving others to flourish in an *embarras de richesse*.

The difference with biological weapons is that they are designed primarily to produce an ecological upset of this kind. The system they are meant to upset is the delicate balance attained between disease-producing organisms and their hosts. The method is simply to introduce into an area millions of infectious organisms that did not exist there before. This, by definition, is bound to upset the prevailing ecological situation. It might, as some scientists have suggested, so alter the balance between microbe and man as to produce a world in which disease once again becomes completely unmanageable. If so, we would be plunged back into the Dark Ages of medical practice and, by implication, into the prehuman era of social behavior. Under such circumstances, it would be small consolation that our airports and railways, our towns and cities, our factories and parliaments were left standing. Biological weapons may well be "nondestructive" of property, but they are certainly destructive of all that we value as human.

THE SILENT WEAPONS

CHAPTER 1

Plowshares into Swords

Beat your plowshares into swords, and your pruning-hooks into spears: let the weak say, I am strong.

JOEL 3:10

THE IDEA of using toxic chemicals and disease-producing organisms to win battles is not new. What is new is the intensity of the effort now being made to develop these weapons and the attitude of defense officials toward their use. For whereas ten years ago, twenty years ago, and fifty years ago they were regarded as the worst form of military brutality that could be employed on the battle-field, military officials are now arguing that these weapons could be the most humane ever invented. That is not to say that they are being so intensively developed for that reason; on the contrary, chemical weapons, at least, are being developed because of their military value—the type of war in which the United States has become involved in Vietnam, for instance, is one in which chemicals can be used with effect. But the military have used the argument that these weapons are humane in a successful attempt to secure greater sums of money for their development. In this decade their success in this field has brought about a new weapons escalation, a new threat to world peace, and a new flouting of one of the few interna-

1

tional agreements in existence to limit the types of weapons to be used in war.

The current concern with chemical and biological weapons is a direct reflection of the means scientists have been devising to fight crop pests. This may sound strange, but the history of weapons technology has always been closely connected with food gathering. Whether the first bow and arrow were invented to hunt game or keep the neighbors under control is not known; but the weapon was certainly used for both purposes. Today we rely heavily on toxic chemicals for the maintenance of our food supplies and agriculture has become thoroughly adapted to the routine and massive use of insecticides and herbicides to improve its yields. Many of these chemicals have similarities to those that have been developed for exterminating not pests but men. It was during the hunt for better insecticides that the Germans, in the late 1930s, stumbled upon the most toxic of all the chemical weapons that are currently stockpiled: the nerve gases. But the agriculturists have also been seeking more biological means of controlling predators since before the turn of the century. They have tried spraying caterpillars with suspensions of virus and bacteria. And they have virtually eliminated the rabbit population in many parts of the world by disseminating the virus disease known as myxomatosis among the rabbits and the fleas which carry the virus.

The aims of chemical and biological warfare are remarkably similar to these agricultural efforts. Just as the agriculturists have available a huge range of chemicals to treat every conceivable agricultural need, so too have the defense departments of at least the Soviet Union and the United States an equally large range of chemicals stockpiled for use in wars to come. The chemical weapons are well developed and are ready for use, whether it be on jungle, on pasture land, or on the battlefield. But the biological weapons are not so well developed. Just as the agriculturists have found greater difficulties in preparing effective biological weapons, so, too, have defense departments. But the explosive outbreak of myxomatosis should give us pause. If biological control can be used in this way against the rabbit population, we should not be too confident that it could not be used equally effectively against the human population. The world is making every effort to turn its "plowshares and pruninghooks" into weapons far sharper than the sword and the spear.

The surprising thing, perhaps, is that the systematic use of chemicals in agriculture has produced a more vocal protest, and a much more cleverly argued one, than have the preparations to use similar chemicals against man. No one has considered this problem in anything like the detail in which Rachel Carson, in her *Silent Spring,* examined the agricultural problem. It is true, of course, that when chemical weapons were first used in World War I they produced a wide range of emotional reaction. Hysterical headlines in the newspapers have followed every subsequent use of gas in war that has been recorded. But few people have probed the situation in much more depth. There has been little mention of the insidious stockpiling and development of antipersonnel chemicals, and there has been little enlightened public discussion of their possible military roles or of the effects they might produce. This weapon is every bit as devastating in its potential destructive capability as the nuclear stockpile. And yet it is almost disregarded at the tables of the disarmament conferences.

In this book I shall try to throw some light on the objectives of toxic warfare, the types of weapon which are or may become feasible, and the potential dangers they represent. But I shall have to disappoint some readers straight away. This book is not an exposé; it contains no classified information. It does, I hope, paint a picture that is both reasonably accurate and certainly alarming of the current state of the art of chemical and biological warfare.

Nor, I am afraid, is this a book for those who are not prepared to consider the issues involved fairly dispassionately. The old World War I emotional reaction against chemical warfare will no longer do. If, optimistically, we are going to learn to control this weapon, we shall have to sharpen our arguments for rejecting it. If, pessimistically, we are going to learn to live with it, as we have the nuclear weapon, we need to know a good deal more about it. The emotional reaction may be instinctively right but it is logically wrong. Many weapons are more horrifying in their effects than the chemical ones. This emotional attitude may in the past have done some good—it was certainly responsible, at least in part, for ensuring that chemical weapons remained unused virtually for the entire half-century from 1917 to 1967. But it has also done some harm. It has been mainly responsible for frightening the authorities into concealing their efforts in this area under cloak-and-dagger security. The public knows far more about the mechanisms of the hydrogen bomb, the extent of the nations' nuclear stockpiles, and the methods of delivering nuclear warheads than they do about the technology of chemical warfare. Yet there is no basic reason why this should be. Every effort to conceal weapon development makes a potential enemy that much more suspicious; it makes him increase his efforts in the same field of development; and, by heightening international tension, it brings the possibility of war just that much nearer.

The military arguments for developing chemical and

biological weapons run roughly as follows. They offer the possibility of taking enemy strongholds or territory without destroying property, power stations, communications networks, roads, or bridges in that territory. They are cheap to produce, particularly when compared with nuclear weapons. They are also cheaper to deliver. They provide a new weapon in the spectrum that is already available; they provide, it is argued, something midway between the conventional weapon and the ultimate use of the hydrogen bomb. Biological weapons are particularly cheap in that the victim is made to do most of the work. All that is needed is a small quantity of highly virulent and infectious viruses or bacteria that can be sprayed, living, into the atmosphere. As soon as a few living particles are inhaled, they multiply in the host's body, eventually producing the symptoms of disease. Because they multiply so quickly only a very small dose is needed to spread infection through large populations. It could be dropped by aircraft, spread by saboteurs via a reservoir or ventilation system, and even spread by animals that carry the disease naturally. No expensive force of nuclear bombers or submarines would be required. Military enthusiasts have often described this cheap, "nondestructive" method of warfare as the panacea of future military conflict.

As we shall see, a good many of these arguments do not hold up under close examination. And there is, of course, another side to this issue. These weapons are potentially capable of producing huge numbers of civilian casualties and have been internationally banned in war. These alone are two good reasons for not using them. Furthermore, there is no hard and fast means of deciding what is a chemical weapon and what a biological one—for technical reasons, the types of weapon merge into one another.

This means that the first use of chemical warfare could escalate into a biological war. And biological weapons have never yet been used on a large scale. We do not know from experience exactly what the results would be like, and we are not yet able to predict such things with any accuracy. They would certainly depend a good deal on prevailing meteorological conditions. The effect might be negligible. Equally, it could produce casualties on a far wider scale than anything that has ever occurred before. Even worse, it might give rise to serious ecological effects, possibly affecting the overall balance of nature, which is easily enough disturbed, irreversibly. The introduction of large numbers of any living organism into a region is one of the surest ways of destroying the equilibrium which nature has striven for millenniums to attain.

There are also moral reasons for refraining from the use of biological warfare. For one thing, disease attacks the weakest members of a population first. The women and children, the aged, the sick, and the dying—these will be the first to succumb. Biological warfare is essentially warfare against civilians, for these are normally the weakest members of any nation at war. The troops, too, are likely to have better methods of protecting themselves against biological attack.

We shall be considering all these questions in more detail later on in this book. In the next chapter I shall say something about the historical picture, and the activities of the first half of this century. But to make it quite plain that this is not all a storm in a tea cup, I would like to anticipate myself somewhat by describing the current American research, development, and production program in chemical and biological warfare. By doing this I do not intend to imply that the Americans are more to blame than any other nation. But the American program should be the first to be described. For one thing, far more is known about it than about the programs of other countries. For another, it is on a much larger scale than it is, for instance, in the United Kingdom. And, finally, it is the Americans who have recently resorted to chemical warfare on a large scale in Vietnam.

The exact amount of money which the American taxpayer is currently paying for his chemical and biological weapons is not publicly known. It is, however, probably over $300 million a year. This is a lot of money. But it is only a small percentage of the total American defense expenditure. This should not mislead us because chemical and biological weapons, compared with other armaments, are exceedingly cheap. Their "cost-effectiveness" is exceedingly high. So if these forms of warfare take up a fraction of a percent of the defense budget, this does not reflect accurately their importance in the eyes of the officials who are concerned with balancing the budget. They realize full well they are getting a good bargain.

The U.S. center for research into biological warfare is known as Fort Detrick and it is situated near Frederick, Maryland. It has 1,300 acres of ground and employs nearly 700 scientifically trained personnel. Some 15 percent of the work it does finds its way into the published literature; the rest is classified by the Department of Defense, although some of it is also available to other nations. In character it is much like any other large biological research center. It has an animal farm to provide the subject matter of experimental tests and the standard equipment of any microbiological laboratory. But its objectives are totally different. The offensive departments at Detrick —and the laboratory is concerned with both offense and defense—seek out ways of making microorganisms more infectious, less susceptible to drugs and antibiotics, and

able to survive for longer periods when released in the atmosphere. The work represents a fundamental denial of
all that doctors have been trained to achieve; it is a research effort which flies in the face of medicine itself.

Detrick is only one of many laboratories and plants
engaged full time on the chemical and biological warfare
business. The equivalent of Detrick on the chemical side
is the Edgewood Arsenal in Maryland. Work here includes both the manufacture of weapons and the business
of filling munitions with the materials to be used. Other
chemicals are produced at the Rocky Mountain Arsenal
in Denver and, until recently, at yet another plant in
Muscle Shoals, Alabama. At an estimated annual cost
of $3.5 million, a plant at Newport, Indiana, produces
one of the nerve gases and has rockets, mines, and shells
filled with the chemical. The plant is said to have been
operating daily, on a 24-hour basis, since 1960. Both
chemical and biological weapons are tested at the Dugway
Proving Ground in Utah which employs about 900 people
and occupies more ground than the state of Rhode Island.
(Twelve senior British officers attend a course there every
year.) Another unit, the Pine Bluff Arsenal in Arkansas,
is concerned with the manufacture of both chemical and
biological weapons, although it is not known whether it
does in fact actually produce biological ones.

The equipment is there. The organization is there. The
chemical munitions, at least, are also there. But this is by
no means the end of the story. In two brilliant articles for
Science (January 13 and 20, 1967) Elinor Langer probed
the relationship which universities and other institutions
had with chemical and biological warfare. She claimed,
for instance, that during a ten-year period Johns Hopkins
University received more than $1 million for a research
contract, which included a study of the diseases that were

of potential significance in biological warfare. Work at the University of Pennsylvania has involved an analysis of the effects of various chemical and biological weapons on humans, and their response to a "chemical and biological warfare environment." Also involved, according to Langer, have been Duke University Medical Center, Stanford University, Brooklyn College, New York Botanical Gardens, the Midwest Research Institute, the Southern Research Institute, the University of Maryland, the Illinois Institute of Technology, Hahnemann Medical College, the Universities of Chicago, Minnesota, Michigan, and Texas, Ohio State University, the Massachusetts Institute of Technology, the George Washington University, and the University of Utah. Doubtless this list could be considerably lengthened. By some particularly perverse stroke of administration, even the U.S. Public Health Service cooperates with Detrick in a number of ways. Unofficial reports have since suggested that more than 50 American universities and colleges have received contracts for work on chemical and biological warfare.

But if the universities are heavily involved, industry is more so. Even though many of these universities, as well as the established military organizations and other institutions which I have not mentioned, take a sizable amount from the budget for chemical and biological warfare, at times more than 65 percent of the total budget has gone to industry—for a variety of purposes ranging from the routine screening of compounds of possible military significance to the development of specific items of equipment. In other words, American involvement with these weapons reaches most forms of academic and industrial institution. In the United States chemical and biological warfare is apparently both big business and higher learning.

It is clear that these weapons are being developed, that they are being developed fast and seriously, and that they are also being stockpiled. But does the United States intend using them? She alone among the major powers has not ratified the Geneva Protocol, which, in somewhat more precise terms, forbids the use of chemical or biological weapons in warfare. But in 1943 President Roosevelt stated categorically that "we shall under no circumstances resort to the use of such weapons unless they are first used by our enemies." At that time the policy was clear. Since then it has become progressively less clear, unless we interpret the current use of tear gas and herbicides in Vietnam as a direct denial of Roosevelt's policy.

This "no first use" policy was somewhat more loosely reaffirmed by Eisenhower in 1960. But by the end of that year a member of the House of Representatives proposed a resolution to Congress that chemical weapons should not be used by the United States in a war unless they were first used by an enemy. The resolution was opposed by the State and Defense Departments, and it was defeated. If further evidence of what the current situation is should be required, it remains only to quote from the U.S. Army Field Manual FM 27-10, "The Law of Land Warfare." It reads: "The United States is not a party to any treaty, now in force, that prohibits or restricts the use in warfare of toxic or nontoxic gases, of smoke or incendiary materials, or of bacteriological warfare." Officials who have been asked to re-affirm Roosevelt's no first use policy have recently declined to do so. Their actions in Vietnam suggest to most of us that that policy is no longer in force. For the Americans to argue that what is going on in Vietnam is not chemical warfare is only a verbal quibble. And if history is anything to go by, this action will in any case soon

lead to actions which all of us would call chemical warfare.

As Elinor Langer has concluded: "The United States
Government is developing chemical and biological weapons. It is learning how to use them effectively. And, finally,
it is inquiring into the public reaction to their use." We
have much less evidence, but I feel sure that similar remarks would apply to the Soviet Union. And, I suspect, to
a number of smaller countries who see in the cheapness of
chemical and biological warfare a means of rivaling the
nuclear killing power of their larger neighbors.

CHAPTER 2

"War Without Death"

There is such a thing as legitimate warfare; war has its laws; there are things which may fairly be done, and things which may not be done. . . . he has attempted (as I may call it) to *poison the wells.*

Cardinal Newman, 1864

CHEMICAL or biological weapons have been used in war for a good deal longer than history has been recorded. Medea and Circe, the daughters of the Greek goddess Hecate, were worshipped as poisoners and it was with the help of one of Medea's concoctions that Jason is said to have won his kingdom. Even in legend, then, man was familiar with the use of poison not just for solving family problems but for dealing with enemies on a fairly large scale. Poisoned arrows have been used for almost as long as the bow and arrow.

This, perhaps, is an appropriate place to clear up misunderstandings about what is meant by chemical warfare. A military chemical industry first grew up with the invention of gunpowder. But these are not the kinds of substance with which we shall be concerned in this book. Chemical and biological weapons have one important property in common: they are both toxic. Incendiary chemicals, flame throwers, napalm, and the like could be

12

called toxic, but they depend for their effect on properties other than toxicity. The results they produce may be even more horrifying than those of toxic weapons but they are essentially rather small-scale weapons when compared to the enormous potential killing power of highly toxic materials. Of course, this business of toxicity can also be rather confusing for a dictionary defines the term "as anything which has a harmful effect on a living organism." Under this definition even water could be described as toxic for it will certainly produce harmful effects if drunk in large enough quantities. But let us not get bogged down in semantic detail; henceforth we shall be dealing with what you and I commonly understand to be toxic materials, whether they are living bacteria or synthetic insecticides.

The use of primitive types of toxic weapon is also ancient. One of the oldest recorded uses was in 600 B.C. when the great Athenian legislator Solon had roots of helleborus thrown into a small river which his enemy used as drinking water. The result was a violent attack of diarrhea among his opponents, which led to their defeat. In 200 B.C. a Carthaginian general played a clever tactical game with his enemy. Retreating from his camp as an apparent sign of impending defeat, he left behind a large stock of wine which he had treated with mandragora, a toxic root which produces narcotic effects when ingested. During the enemy's prolonged and deep sleep which followed, the Carthaginian army returned to the camp and slew them.

This action might now be classified as biological war, for it involved the use of chemicals produced not synthetically but by living organisms. In any event, an undoubted use of biological warfare was to follow only 16 years later. In a naval battle against Eumenes II of Pergamum, Hannibal ordered earthenware pots filled with snakes to be lobbed onto the decks of the enemy ships. The resulting confusion cost the Pergamene sailors a defeat.

From this time on, the poisoning of water supplies and wine and food became a progressively more common weapon of war. One of the most effective tricks was to throw the decaying bodies of animals or soldiers into a well which the enemy used to obtain drinking water. In 1155, for instance, the Emperor Frederick Barbarossa took the Italian town of Tortuna by poisoning its water supplies in this way. In fact, to make doubly sure of his victory, he also resorted to chemical warfare, adding to the water burning torches of tar and sulphur, which made it virtually undrinkable.

The deliberate spread of disease in war is more difficult to date, for all armies—as they do today—suffer greatly from naturally occurring disease. Indeed, this was often a more serious threat to their survival than the still primitive weapons of their enemies. During the Crusades, certainly, biological warfare was extensively practiced and the plague-ridden bodies of one side would often be introduced into the camps of the other side in an effort to spread the disease further. How effective this tactic was is difficult to tell, because, as we shall see, plague conquered most of Europe in the space of a very few years in the 14th century without any deliberate human intervention.

There seems to be no doubt, however, that biological warfare was used against the American Indians by the early European colonists. Before the arrival of the white man smallpox was unknown to the Indian and he had acquired no natural immunity to it. It was soon spread naturally from the invading forces to the totally unprotected native population, and quickly produced millions of deaths. But deliberate attempts were also made to encourage the spread of smallpox. Sir Jeffrey Amherst, who was Commander in Chief of the British forces in America in 1763, had two blankets and a handkerchief from a British smallpox hospital sent to Indian chiefs with the result that an attack of smallpox soon broke out.

America was also the scene of biological warfare during the Civil War. It was accepted practice on both sides during that war to contaminate or pollute any water hole or stream before vacating an area. In July 1863, for instance, General Johnston who was retreating from Vicksburg being followed by General Sherman, filled ponds and lakes with the bodies of both pigs and sheep.

It is often said that the world has not yet seen biological warfare practiced. From what I have just said, this is clearly not strictly true. What is true, however, is that biological warfare has never been used on the scale that is now possible in the 20th century. In history it was often a last resort, a clever idea or simply an afterthought. It was always an auxiliary weapon and used with great clumsiness and without any proper understanding of what was involved. These characteristics are so different from the way in which biological weapons might be used today that it is quite fair to refer to biological warfare as an untried means of waging war. When, and if, it is first used on a large and systematic scale it will be only too apparent just how important these factors of sophistication and knowledge have become.

But the modern form of chemical warfare was certainly conceived in the 19th century. In 1855 the British War Department was shown shells filled with cacodyl and cacodyl oxide—substances containing arsenic—mixed with a self-inflammable material, which were presumably intended to produce an equivalent of the arsenic smokes that were to be used in World War I. At this time, too, the

British General Dundonald suggested that sulphur dioxide should be used in the siege of Sebastopol. But his application was rejected by the Government. In the States in 1862, it was suggested that chlorine be used in the Civil War but again the offer was not taken up (chlorine was one of the first gases to be used in World War I). And during the Boer War the British were convinced that their wells had been poisoned with potassium cyanide—an extremely fast-acting lethal poison. It seems more than dubious that this was a correct diagnosis, for the British Medical Staff recommended antidotes for the poisoning, which normally occurs far too quickly for any treatment to be given.

Early in the 20th century, however, chemical warfare evolved into an important tactical weapon. Since then there has been a continuous development of chemical weapons which I will describe in more detail in the next chapter. For the rest of this chapter I shall deal with the continued growth of interest in biological weapons, which have still not reached the state of military preparedness that chemicals had by the end of World War I.

Precisely when modern biological warfare was first treated seriously by military and political thinkers is not known. Presumably it was at some stage early in this century when, of course, it was referred to as bacteriological warfare because the true nature of viruses had not been established. As I have said, no one has admitted yet to waging biological war in the manner in which scientists now believe it might be waged. So what follows is an account of the various allegations that have been made and the preparations that nations have made to put themselves in a position from which they could both defend themselves against biological attack and utilize it if it seemed desirable. These allegations may or may not be true and for the most part I doubt their veracity. But this is not perhaps the point. What is important is that quite early in this century military leaders became very much aware of the potentialities of biological warfare. The accusations of the misuse of biological science in this way show us something of the thinking about the subject at that time. They show us, too, that this is no new phenomenon and that, certainly during the Second World War, the risk of biological attack was held to be quite high.

The first definite allegation was in 1915 when it was claimed that German agents had inoculated horses and cattle that were leaving the United States for Allied ports with disease producing organisms. The type of bacterium used was not detailed but allegations a year or so later were more specific. The bacteria that cause anthrax and glanders—two animal diseases that can also be contracted by humans and of which we shall be hearing a good deal in this book—were said to be inoculated into horses and cattle at Bucharest in Roumania in 1916, and on the French front in 1917 where some 4,500 donkeys became infected with glanders. These instances have been referred to many times in the literature on the subject but, even if they are correct in substance, they certainly played no major part in the war and had a negligible effect on its outcome. Even less substantiated are the wild allegations that were made in the United States in 1919 when that country was suffering particularly heavily from the worldwide influenza pandemic that was then at its height. Several newspapers ran stories pointing an accusing finger at the Germans for initiating the outbreak but this was vigorously denied from all quarters, including the American government. If the pandemic had been less crippling, these allegations might have been treated more seriously. As it was, the governments were so concerned

with the vast effects of the pandemic on national econo-
mies and morale that they had little time for these more
political issues. Their main concern was to prevent public
panic in the biggest outbreak of disease which the world
has ever known.

Much later, in the 1930s, allegations were made that the
Germans had tried to spread cholera in Italy during the
First World War. This gained no substantiation but in
1934 a British journalist, Wickham Steed, exposed what
he believed to be German experiments to propagate the
bacterium *Serratia marcescens* in the underground railways of London and Paris. These experiments were said to
be continued under Hitler's orders in Paris. But though
Steed claimed the experiments were initiated in 1931 these
activities were never taken very seriously by officials and
did not feature in the Nuremberg War Trials as they would
most surely have done if they could have been substantiated.

But by this time the threat of a Second World War was
becoming plain to many nations. To many of them, too, it
seemed as though this coming war would see the first use
of biological weapons on a large scale. Earlier, in 1925, a
clause had been incorporated into the Geneva Protocol
prohibiting the use of bacteriological warfare. Even in
those days this was a serious enough threat to warrant international legislation.

Of the major nations involved in the Second World War,
we know that the United States, Britain, Canada, Germany, and Japan gave serious consideration to biological
weapons. Fortunately, these weapons were never used—if
they were actually prepared—although it was established
to the satisfaction of the Soviet Extraordinary Commission
that the Germans had made deliberate efforts to spread
typhus among both Soviet civilians and troops. This ac-

cusation was not taken up, and few further details of German activity in this field have ever been released. Detailed reports have been compiled of what the Germans were up to but they have never been released to the public.

A more detailed account of American work in this field is available, thanks mainly to the writings of Dr. Theodor Rosebury who worked until 1946 at Fort Detrick, the American center for research into biological warfare. Rosebury has said that under the stress of the Second World War it seemed advisable to some scientists, who would otherwise have found such work morally repugnant, to become involved in at least the defense aspects of biological warfare. He himself left Detrick promptly after the war and has since attacked current efforts in the field from a variety of moral standpoints. During the 1940s and 1950s he did perhaps more than anyone to alert the public conscience to the dangers of biological warfare and the efforts which the United States in particular was still expending in peacetime to promote the state of the art.

By the end of World War II about 5,000 people were employed at Fort Detrick. Many of them, it is true, were engaged ostensibly in defensive roles but tests of biological weapons were carried out on an island in Mississippi Sound and at the Army Proving Ground in Dugway, Utah. Although biological weapons were not actually being manufactured, a plant had been built in Indiana for the production of *Bacillus globigii,* a harmless bacterium. Doubtless the plant could equally well have been used to produce less harmless organisms for even if the details differ the operating principles by which one cultures bacteria are the same regardless of species. However, the intention at the Indiana plant was not to produce pathogenic organisms until the safety of the plant had been established and its operators trained.

In Britain the effort was on a much smaller scale for the total labor force at the Microbiological Research Establishment in Porton, Wiltshire, was only 45 people, of whom 15 were scientists led by the Director Dr. Paul Fildes. The M.R.E. was the nearest equivalent there was in the United Kingdom to Fort Detrick. One of the most notable activities of this unit during the war was an experiment carried out on Gruinard Island, off the northwest coast of mainland Scotland. It involved spraying the island with anthrax bacteria and was apparently conducted to test the feasibility of biological warfare. The victims of this particular experiment were sheep and the current director of the M.R.E., Dr. C. E. Gordon Smith, has said that this experiment was instrumental in persuading experts that a biological warfare attack was a feasible military proposition. Certainly, from then on the British have taken biological warfare seriously. The biological activities at Porton did not, however, receive a great deal of publicity with the exception of a field test that was made in 1954 in the Bahamas area and the unfortunate death of one of their staff from plague in 1962.

The Japanese effort is probably the best documented of any, partly as a result of a Soviet trial of 12 Japanese prisoners in 1949 for preparing and employing biological weapons during the war and partly as a result of the publication of the findings of an International Scientific Commission, which was called in to report when the Chinese and North Koreans accused the Americans of resorting to biological warfare in China and Korea. Reports of the Soviet trial revealed that the Japanese effort in biological warfare had started in 1931. Two installations were built in 1936 in Manchuria (then in Japanese territory), one of which was situated near Harbin. A Japanese writer was later described by *The New York Times* (July 16,

1955) as having witnessed tests in which 1,500 to 2,000 human guinea pigs died as a result of biological warfare experiments at a center near Harbin. This was disguised as a Red Cross Unit and was hurriedly destroyed in 1945 when the Russians joined the war in that area.

The men tried at Khabarovsk in 1949 were all military prisoners and included the former Commander in Chief of the Kwantung Army. At this trial it was "established" that the Japanese had made attacks with plague on China, and the Chinese report which I have mentioned states that these attacks produced about 700 deaths between 1940 and 1944. The Japanese centers, according to the proceedings of the Khabarovsk trial, were working on three lines of bacteriological warfare. One concerned the dropping of bombs from aircraft, another the spraying of bacteria from aircraft, and the third means of contaminating water sources and land by sabotage. The actual diseases being investigated included plague, cholera, typhoid, paratyphoid, and anthrax. Chinese and Soviet prisoners were said to have been used in experiments, and attacks against the Chinese were claimed to have been made that involved both plague and paratyphoid.

During the late 1940s and 1950s the Soviet Union tried on a number of occasions to make political capital out of accusations that noncommunist countries, the United States in particular, were experimenting with biological warfare. In a sense this was not surprising, both because of the political atmosphere at the time and because of the Americans' own commitments in this field— which were, incidentally, to become much larger by the early 1960s. Typical of these accusations was one made in 1949 that the Americans, in an experimental test, had produced an epidemic among the Canadian Eskimos by means of a biological weapon. Rosebury has said that the wide publicity given to biological warfare during this time was favorable to wild speculation in the press about where and when it was used. British papers, for instance, claimed that the Germans had planned to send an ultimatum to the Americans and British backed up by the threat of "deadly germ warfare." And in 1947 an American commentator blamed the Soviet Union for the Egyptian cholera outbreak of 1947 (the Americans helped fight this epidemic by having cholera vaccine flown in). Such accusations do not warrant serious consideration but the Khabarovsk trial is rather different. For one thing it involved the Japanese. For another, much of what was reported there was confirmed by the International Scientific Commission, which investigated the Chinese and Korean allegations (admittedly one member of the Commission had been chief medical expert at the Khabarovsk trial, so this coincidence may not be entirely fortuitous).

In 1952 the International Scientific Commission was called in by the Academia Sinica and the Chinese Peace Committee to investigate allegations that had been made by the Chinese and the North Koreans that the United States had been engaged in biological warfare in these areas. The six members of the commission were internationally known scientists from a variety of countries. Dr. Joseph Needham was the only British member of the Commission. Its members spent several weeks in the summer of 1952 visiting the "attacked" areas and talking to local witnesses. They heard how American planes had been seen or heard flying over almost every area which subsequently recorded an outbreak of unusual disease and how on some occasions objects were seen falling through the air, sometimes accompanied by an unpleasant smell of burning skin or horn. They claimed to have found unusually high concentrations of insects appearing in these regions, which were either unknown locally or which appeared in anomalous seasons. Furthermore, the Commission found that various insects appeared in the region on a time scale that was quite unlike their natural order of appearance. Insects that would normally appear relatively late in the season were found to have been recorded earlier than other insects which would have been expected under natural conditions to occur early in the season. Nearly all the allegations concerned not the spraying of aerosols of bacteria but the dropping of disease-infected animals and objects. Among those mentioned were plague-infected fleas and voles, anthrax-infected feathers and cholera-infected clams (the latter in the neighborhood of water reservoirs; cholera is normally transmitted via contaminated water).

Exactly what effect these and other agents had on the local populations was not revealed although the report did stress that thanks to the rapid advance of Chinese public hygiene outbreaks of disease were kept to a minimum. The local people, the report claimed, kept calm throughout the attacks and this also helped to prevent any massive outbreak of disease. Throughout their report, the Commission were at pains to point to the similarities between the types of biological warfare which they claimed had been waged and the known development of Japanese biological warfare research in the previous decade. They reproduced facsimile pages of an article on biological warfare written by a former Major in the Epidemic Prevention Service of the Japanese Kwantung Army, which appeared in the *Sunday Mainichi* on January 27, 1952. In this article, Sakaki Ryohei, the author, described biological warfare as a real military threat and discussed means by which biological weapons could be disseminated. Included in the article were diagrams of the types of container that could be used. Some were equipped with a parachute to slow their descent, some broke open on impact with the ground, and one illustration showed a container for delivering plague-infected rats.

The implication behind all this stemmed, of course, from the fact that after the Japanese were defeated in 1945 at least one of the Japanese centers that had conducted research into biological warfare fell into American hands. The allegation was that the Americans were trying out what they had learned from the Japanese. Needless to say, the Americans denied the allegation vigorously and most of the Western world came to their defense. There is little doubt in the minds of any of the experts on biological war to whom I have talked in the United Kingdom that the allegations were unfounded and were trumped up charges used to heighten international tension over the Korean conflict. If the Americans had wanted to use biological warfare, they would, it is claimed, have made a much better job of it than appeared to be the case. Certainly they would not have relied upon animal carriers or vectors to spread the disease for even in the early 1950s it was realized that this was an unreliable method of dissemination and that the spraying of biological aerosols would be a more effective means of waging biological warfare. But this was not an argument which appealed to Chinese sympathizers because they felt the Americans could simply be using the area as a proving ground—as they are also alleged to have done in Vietnam—to demonstrate to themselves that this technique of biological warfare did not work. The Commission itself anticipated this very query, in fact. They concluded simply that the idea that animal vectors could not be used to spread disease was a mistaken one; and they mentioned their suspicion that a biological aerosol had been used to start an epidemic of encephalitis.

Another argument against the Commission, which was used even by nonpolitical parties, was that its members did not constitute the most objective or highly qualified personnel who could have been chosen for the job. Several members of the Commission were internationally known for their interest in Chinese affairs. Not all of them could be claimed to be real experts in biological warfare techniques. The report would certainly have had a better reception if the scientists involved had been more experienced in the field concerned and less politically biased.

The scientific content came in for less public criticism, although I have heard experts argue that it does not add up to a very compelling case. But the Commission certainly made one glaring error if its objective was to convince the world that the Americans really had been using biological warfare. This was the inclusion in the report of the "confessions" of American airmen who had been captured on the flights in which these biological bombs were said to have been dropped. The titles of three of these confessions speak for themselves: "The Truth About How American Imperialism Launched Germ Warfare"; "How I Was Forced to Take Part in the Inhuman Bacteriological Warfare Launched by the U.S. Wall Street"; and "This Inhuman Warfare Must Be Stopped." The confessions continue in this vein at great length and in considerable detail. But it is difficult to believe they were freely given. They were clearly made under pressure and when the captured pilots returned home they admitted this and recanted their statements. So, it was argued, if the

political half of this report has been faked, what evidence
is there that the same does not apply to the scientific sec-
tions? The Chinese lost heavily by their insistence in having such propaganda included in the report. Without it,
the report, which was published in Prague and dis-
patched free to prominent scientists and politicians
throughout the world, would have had an unquestionably
less hostile reception.

But if we accept this report as mere propaganda, it
is only fair to look more closely at the American literature
of this time, or rather slightly later, to redress the balance.
Up to the late 1950s the American investment in chemical
and biological warfare was relatively small. This was in
spite of a small but vociferous group, centered on the
Army Chemical Corps of World War II, which maintained that their weapons were those of the future and
that they could offer humane and cheap warfare for a long
time to come—if they were given more money to expand
their research program. They launched what was later
admitted to be a publicity program in which they tried to
gain the confidence, by means of their "humane weapons"
story, of newspapers, scientific societies, and above all of
Congress. This piece of publicity went under the name of
"Operation Blue Skies." They advertised, as Elinor Langer
has put it, "war without death." Thanks mainly to the
perspicacity of American newspapermen, the campaign
won relatively little success in the public domain. Indeed,
several publications ran stories exposing the whole move
for the tasteless propaganda that it really was.

One way in which this publicity campaign manifested
itself was at a national meeting of the American Chemical
Society held in April 1960. Rather than try to summarize
this conference myself I think it better to quote in full a
letter published by John Barden in *Bulletin of the Atomic*

Scientists in February 1961.* He managed to summarize the main lectures and the attitude of mind of those who delivered them with a lightness of touch which was apparently totally missing from the conference itself:

Dear Sir:

Last April I dropped in on proceedings of the 137th national meeting of the American Chemical Society, called Symposium on Nonmilitary Defense—Chemical and Biological Defenses in Perspective. We met in a lecture room of Cleveland's Public Hall, a place old enough to smell of disinfectant, which was under the circumstances faintly reassuring.

Dr Harold C. Lueth of the American Medical Association was describing the signs of invisible, odorless, tasteless nerve gas. Early symptoms include headache, blurring of vision, tightness of the chest, and dizziness. Rapidly there will develop severe headache, profuse salivation, tightness and pain in the chest, nausea, vomiting, dimness of vision, early fatigue, drowsiness, cyanosis, collapse, convulsions, and—a shrug passed the case from medical jurisdiction—death may supervene.

Still, nerve gas is painless at the outset, and one runs through the dismal symptoms in less than ten minutes, surely nicer than the way most of us fritter away years, each one closer to the grave. On the whole, I didn't think Dr Lueth, splendid though he was as the medical union's emissary, made the most of his material.

The happy fact that chemical and biological warfare does not destroy property was given a good deal of quiet iteration during the proceedings, telling off the rival vested interests in thermonuclear warfare pretty effectively, I thought. For instance, Dr LeRoy D. Fothergill, who advises the Commanding General, Chemical Warfare, said,

* "Comments on Biological Warfare" by John Barden is reprinted from the February 1961 issue of the *Bulletin of the Atomic Scientists*. Copyright 1961 by the Education Foundation for Nuclear Science.

"An attractive feature of anti-crop warfare is that it does not destroy man's physical assets—his cities, his bridges, his railroads, et cetera."

This attractive feature could solve every vexing problem about property I have been able to think of, namely, the people who have it and the people who don't. The solution is applicable on a continental scale or soon will be. Dr Fothergill, whose look of mildly distressed inquisitiveness was perpetual in these proceedings, told us he had sprayed a cloud of fluorescent particles from a ship at sea with significant success. The ship's run was just 156 miles; 450 pounds of detectable material were used; the wind as part of the calculations carried the cloud over 34,800 square miles of United States territory. The remaining problems are hardly technological, merely quantitative, and nearly everybody can multiply. Title to real estate like the United States and the Soviet Union could be made free and clear, except for bugs and chemicals, give or take a few inconsequential millions sick and dying. Yet neither the Americans nor the Soviets stand to inherit anything from so resolute a deed, since each could and would do it to the other.

This nice conclusion of the Western World was clear from the remarks of Alan W. Donaldson of the U.S. Public Health Service and Maj. Gen. Marshall Stubbs, Chief Chemical Officer, Department of the Army. U.S. and Soviet defenses against strategic chemical-biological attack are just good enough to detect one and retaliate, yet just bad enough to guarantee, right now, very high losses. The situation will unquestionably continue. The notion that retaliatory power is the best defense was accepted by everybody, like French priests gliding over birth control. The retaliations could be expected to kill off most Europeans as well, leaving the parts of the earth most worth inheriting to the under-privileged peoples. Blessed are the meek, for they shall inherit the earth. Yea, and in the latitudes professing to believe in the Beatitudes!

Chemical and biological warfare was also established

as cheap, cheap, cheap. This was intended as another blow to the thermonuclear set, a note of cheer for the taxpayers, and a warning about the under-privileged who are not meek. Any smalltime dictator with a few bugs, chemicals, pots, bottles, warehouses, sprays, free-booting scientists, and saboteurs can develop and use major quantities of chemical-biological agents. Clifford F. Rassweiler of Johns-Manville Corporation mentioned Castro's Cuba; in fact, Mr Rassweiler, a lean, dramatic fellow himself, had quite a range of talk on this subject. Even the Pentagon is worried about somebody sticking a batch of, say, Asiatic cholera into its ventilating system—but I shouldn't be beastly to the Pentagon. Let's just say the world of Mr Rassweiler and the Pentagon isn't my world, worse luck.

The humanitarianism of gas and disease warfare has been touched upon by others. Reversibility is the basis of this claim. Some gases incapacitate temporarily, according to William H. Summerson, Deputy Commander, Army Chemical Research and Development Command. Mental confusion, irresistible sleep, paralysis, blindness, deafness, lack of balance, persistent tears, diarrhea, or vomiting are all feasible. I remember some persistent cases of diarrhea during World War II, which I entered ingloriously as a member of Manhattan's Squadron A. A handful of truck drivers, including me, halted parts of a regimental convoy at various points in Connecticut for public dashes to the bushes to the amusement of their fellow-soldiers and the distress of the inhabitants. Just what would have happened had the whole regiment, or the whole country been stricken with this reversible affliction does not stagger my imagination at all. Those who wish may call it humane. The real difficulty is that one irreversibly goes on living.

A telling point was also made by whitehaired General Stubbs, who thought enough of his idea to depart from manuscript: "Incapacitating compounds . . . might permit a force to gain its objective without killing or maiming personnel—military or civilian. That is, they get you so they have you to work for them." In the same class would be those recovering from such practical diseases of biological warfare as the plague, typhus, typhoid fever, undulant fever, yellow fever, dengue fever, Q fever, Asiatic cholera, smallpox, malaria, tularemia, dysentery, encephalitis, and pneumonia, all requiring hospitalization. Dr Lueth said US hospital beds are presently available for about 12 million with adequate services and supplies for two to three weeks. By the U.S. census, the population is now more than 180 million. If everybody were infected—the bugs have no trouble seeking out their targets; in fact, they rather like it —the odds against having to live on are 15 to one. I find these odds most humane, though not in ways touched on by others.

It won't do to leave the humane aspects of this type of warfare without mentioning certain protective measures announced by George D. Rich of the Office of Civil and Defense Mobilization. The OCDM has developed prototype gas masks and baby containers for the civilian population. Impermeable family shelters with filter pumps cranked by hand (civilians would live better electrically if they had some electricity, but they won't) are under development. These items will be put into production and sold, profitably, through regular retail channels to paying customers. I thought this was just about the nicest thing emerging from the proceedings. The only possible exception was a remark by Paul Weiss of the Rockefeller Institute: "We must convince the scientific community that chemical and biological warfare is not a dirty business. It is no worse than other means of killing."

JOHN BARDEN

Fenn College
Cleveland, Ohio

But the ear of the American Congressman is not always tuned to the same sophisticated wavelength of the American commentator. One of the results of this publicity program was a report on research in chemical, biological, and radiological warfare that was presented to the House of Representatives on July 27, 1959, by the Committee on Science and Astronautics. This committee had had a few strings pulled in high up places with the result that they were given information and shown film that had not previously been made public. The Chairman of the Committee, in his letter to the Speaker of the House of Representatives, concluded that "the committee . . . wishes to convey the strong sense of urgency it feels that the American people should gain a better understanding of these new weapons." This seemed a praiseworthy enough aim but the report itself soon revealed that it was concerned not so much with public education as with bringing about a climate of opinion in which the American taxpayer could be persuaded to part with a good deal more money to pay for research on chemical and biological weapons. If propaganda is the term for the report of the Korean Committee, it is also the term I would use to describe the conclusion of this report, which contained the following points:

5) There is an urgent need for a higher level of support on a continuing long run basis in order to develop better detection and protection measures against possible employment of CBR weapons against this country.

11) It is also recognized that in the present world situation with other countries pursuing vigorous programs of CBR development, the best immediate guarantee the United States can possess to ensure that CBR is not used anywhere against the free world is to have a strong capability in this field, too. This will only come with a stronger program of research. . . .

12) At the present time, CBR research is supported at a level equivalent to only one-thousandth of our total de-

fense budget. In the light of its potentialities, this committee recommends that serious consideration be given to the request of Defense officials that this support be at least trebled. Only an increase of such size is likely to speed research to a level of attainment compatible with the efforts of the Communist nations.

13) If CBR is to be considered a deterrent force in the US arsenal of weapons, the program of research advocated here will have to be accompanied by an adequate program of manufacture and deployment of CBR munitions.

To make the point quite clear the committee also devoted a section of their report to the activities of the Communists in this field (the facts they produced were trivial but they claimed "security" as a reason for not including details). They emphasized that chemical and biological weapons were cheap and went to great lengths to show how productive research into chemical and biological weapons was in terms of civilian advances. This is the so-called spin-off which the committee described in an appendix of 19 pages of rather small type. The actual report took 16 pages of much larger type.

But, combined with a number of other factors, the report had its effect. It came at the correct psychological moment, at a time of nuclear stalemate and when further American involvement in small wars with small nations seemed imminent. In such campaigns the prospect of "war without death" seemed as attractive to the politicians as the thought of a Soviet lead in chemical and biological warfare techniques seemed unattractive. In short, the campaigners won their way. In 1961 the total research and development program on chemical and biological warfare amounted to $57 million, with the Army having an additional $46 million for the procurement of actual weapons. By 1964 the research and development program was costing rather more than $158 million and all three services had allocations for procurement: the Army $117 million, the Navy $11 million and the Air Force $8.7 million.

This was a rapid turn of events. It did not take people by surprise, for, by the time the extra spending had been agreed upon, discussion of chemical and biological warfare was no longer a political aim. The publicity campaign was quieted down. It arose, as we shall see, from a different quarter when it was revealed that the Americans had begun to use chemical weapons in Vietnam on a massive scale. This was the first time that chemicals had been used extensively in military combat since that first occasion, almost exactly 50 years previously, when the chemical weapon made its spectacular debut in the First World War.

CHAPTER 3

The Chemical Armory

The goal, of course, is to render the enemy incapable
of movement—that is, we would like to be able to paralyze
the voluntary body functions while allowing the involun-
tary to function normally. Lesser effects, however, might
be just as acceptable—for instance, temporary loss of sight
or disruption of normal body functioning by inducing such
things as vomiting, dysentery or various types of food
poisoning.

Albert E. Hayward,
US Directorate of Defense Research and Engineering
(*Missiles and Rockets,* October 5, 1964)

EARLY in World War I there were persistent rumors that
the Germans had invented some new and deadly weapon,
which was likely to be crucial in the war. The rumors
were given little heed by many military commanders although, as it appeared after the war, they stemmed from
statements made by captured German prisoners that the
German war machine had already made extensive preparations for the use of poison gas. As it turned out, the
French were to be the first to use toxic weapons in the
war—tear-gas grenades fired from rifles—and so should
technically be given the unenviable credit for initiating
the use of a weapon that was to cause more than a million
casualties before the war had ended. But the French action, taken in August 1914 soon after the war began, at-

tracted little attention; many of the histories of the First World War which bother to describe gas warfare at all make no mention of it. The full blame for what was to follow is usually given to the Germans.

On October 27, 1914, the Germans ushered in the new age of chemical warfare with a good deal more determination. At Neuve Chappelle in northern France they bombarded the British forces with shrapnel containing a chemical irritant known as dianisidine chlorsulphonate. Three months later, in January 1915, they tried again, this time on the Russian front using a different chemical, xylyl bromide, which causes intense irritation of the eyes. Neither action was a success, mainly because the chemicals could not be dispersed in sufficient concentration and also, in the second attack, because the chemical chosen was a liquid with a high boiling point; the intense cold of a Russian January prevented the liquid's becoming sufficiently vaporized to produce any real effect. But these attacks were not symptomatic of what was to come. They were the first experimental uses in combat of a new form of warfare. These early attacks provided the Germans with the information and experience needed to perfect their newfound weapons. By the time they tried again, they had learned their lessons.

They chose April 22, 1915, a fine spring day, and the vicinity of Langemarck near Ypres as the time and place to prove to the world that the invention of gunpowder was but one step in the evolution of military weapons. Having bombarded the French forces with high explosive since early morning, they halted their fire about two hours before sunset. They then opened more than 500 cylinders containing 168 tons of pressurized chlorine gas and waited as the light wind bore it steadily towards the opposing forces.

The effect was devastating. Chlorine is a greenish-yellow gas with a sharp acrid smell. It causes intense irritation of the lungs and if inhaled in a concentration of more than 1 part in 10,000 for a minute or two causes death. The same concentration is incapacitating if inhaled for only a few seconds. The Germans had released the gas over a four-mile front on an enemy who were totally unprepared for an attack of this kind. All resistance was eliminated on the front to a depth of several miles. There were more than 15,000 casualties including 5,000 fatalities.

Fifty years later it is difficult to tell to what degree the chemical properties of the gas were responsible for this, and to what degree the panic that ensued at first contact with an unknown weapon caused the troops to withdraw so rapidly. In any event, the Germans pushed home their advantage with a second chlorine attack against the Canadians two days later. Within a few days, however, the first respirators had come into military use. Although they consisted initially of pads of cotton waste soaked in sodium thiosulphate (photographic fixer) or sodium carbonate, and only later of simple felt masks, the immediate dangers of novelty and total unpreparedness were over. The first chapter in the history of chemical warfare had ended and, when the second was opened, the boot was on the other foot.

On September 25, 1915, the British released chlorine gas on the Germans at Loos. From then on chlorine gas was used frequently during the war, although it was soon realized that the release of gas from containers was not the most practical means of dispersing chemical agents. For one thing the technique depended critically on meteorological conditions—it involved waiting for the wind to blow in the right direction—and for another it could be used only with a limited number of chemicals such as chlorine. A much better method was to pack the chemical in a shell and arrange for this to burst, scattering its contents over the opposite lines, by incorporating a small explosive charge within the shell. The Germans' first success with this technique was in July 1915 in the Argonne.

From then on chemical escalation began in earnest as, alternately, protective measures were improved and then more effective chemicals were devised to overcome the protection. The first step was the introduction of phosgene, used initially by the Germans in December 1915 and introduced specifically to penetrate the crude gas masks then in existence (technical information on phosgene and other gases is included in Table II). Like chlorine, phosgene is a choking gas but some ten times more toxic in terms of the dose required to incapacitate. Unlike chlorine, however, the effects of phosgene are delayed and symptoms do not appear until several hours after the attack. Once again masks were improved and the Germans retaliated by introducing vomiting gases, such as diphenyl chlorarsine, into the mixture. This was specifically designed to make the enemy take off his mask, which was permeable to this kind of particulate agent. Meanwhile masks improved again and new techniques were devised for delivering a massive dose of chemical that would begin to affect the enemy before they had time to put on their masks. The British developed the Livens projector, a crude form of trench mortar, which delivered a 60-pound bomb containing 30 pounds of phosgene. It was first used at Arras in March 1917.

By modern standards all the toxic chemicals used up to this time would now be considered relatively ineffective, mainly because their toxicity was low and massive quantities of chemical were required to incapacitate. This was not true of the next chemical to be introduced, which has many properties which are still attractive to the military. This was dichlorodiethylsulphide, better known as mustard gas, from the smell of its impure liquid form, or as Yperite from the town of Ypres where it was first used by the Germans in July 1917.

Like many of the toxic "gases," mustard is a liquid at ordinary temperatures, boiling at 217 degrees Centigrade. It evaporates only slowly and in the soil can take weeks to evaporate completely. The liquid itself is harmful, penetrating clothing quite quickly and causing severe, deep burns on the skin, which are difficult to heal. The effects themselves take a few hours to appear but, when they do, they are often widespread. The eyes become inflamed and the lungs irritated. Large doses cause severe vomiting, nausea, fever, and, of course, all the side effects such as shock that result from any severe assault on the human body. Diluted 1 part in 100,000, the gas will produce its effect even with only one or two minutes' exposure. These will begin to appear about an hour after exposure and will be fully developed after perhaps five hours.

It is easy enough to see why mustard gas was so effective. It is practically colorless and odorless, its garlic or mustard smell lasting only a few minutes and occurring only if the material is impure. Providing the means by which the agent is delivered is not discovered, there is little reason why it should be detected until the effects begin to appear some hours later, by which time massive doses may have been received. Furthermore, the liquid and vapor will linger, making any position that has been attacked by mustard untenable for some time. This happened at least twice during World War I, at Bourlon Wood in November 1917 and at Armentières in April 1918. And lastly, although only relatively large doses will produce death, the effects of smaller doses may last for months. To this day there is no adequate treatment for severe mustard burns, and mustard gas or chemical derivatives of it remain the most powerful vesicant or blister agents known. Its great effectiveness during World War I was due mainly to the fact that it broke the gas/gas mask deadlock once and for all. The only perfectly safe defense against mustard gas is an all enveloping suit protecting every square inch of skin. Although such suits are available today, they are somewhat unsatisfactory for technical reasons; early in World War I they were not even available and exposure to mustard gas resulted invariably in large, painful, and incapacitating blisters. During the last year of the war it accounted for 16 percent of the British casualties and 33 percent of the American ones.

During the war more than 3,000 substances were screened for possible use as toxic agents. Far less, however, were actually employed—12 tear gases, 15 choking agents, 3 blood poisons, 4 blister agents, and 4 vomiting gases. Of these, no more than about a dozen produced the intended effect. On both sides, some 125,000 tons of these agents were dispensed by about 17,000 specially trained chemical troops. But mustard gas was never improved upon. In all more than 9 million shells were filled with mustard and they produced some 400,000 casualties. In terms of casualties produced per shell, mustard was roughly five times as effective as either high explosive or shrapnel.

The precise effects of gas warfare are now difficult to assess at all accurately although all the figures published —many of which contradict one another—indicate its importance. For some reason this is not true of many of the books that have been written about World War I— some of which fail to make any mention at all of the use of chemical agents. According to *Encyclopaedia Britannica,* gas caused about 800,000 casualties in all. The breakdown among nations was as follows: the Russians, 275,000 casualties; the French, 190,000; the English, 181,000; the Germans, 78,763; and the Americans, 70,552. The report prepared by the Committee on Science and Astronautics for the U.S. House of Representatives in 1959 puts the total number of casualties in the war at 1,300,000. Probably we shall never be able to establish an exact figure because the records made by the Germans were subsequently destroyed.

The most important point about these statistics is the relative numbers of deaths to casualties. Of the possible total casualties of 1,300,000 only 91,000 deaths have been recorded. In other words the ratio of deaths to casualties may have been as low as 7 percent—roughly one quarter the figure for conventional weapons.

I shall examine the implications of these and other figures in more detail in Chapter 10. All that need be said for the moment is that they have been used to pressurize governments into providing increased funds for research into chemical warfare; the argument is that, as the chemical agents used in World War I produced proportionately far fewer deaths, chemical warfare must be an intrinsically more humane method of warfare. One should remember, however, that the chemicals used in World War I were far less toxic than those that could be used today. There is no evidence that either side deliberately withheld the use of any agent of a highly toxic and lethal nature. The truth is that the chemical technology of the time was not sufficiently advanced to produce an effective and highly lethal agent. Had one been available—as there now is—there is no reason to believe that it would not have been used. If it had, the ratio of deaths to casualties would have been very much higher.

World War I is the best documented case of the use of toxic agents; indeed it is the only war in which toxic agents have been used on a really large scale. Mustard gas was introduced by the Italians against the Abyssinians in January 1936 and proved particularly effective at Mykale because the Abyssinians fought in bare feet. The Japanese also made repeated but small gas attacks against the Chinese in the period 1937 to 1943 using lewisite, mustard, and phenyldichloroarsine. These agents proved particularly useful during the recapture of Ichang on the Yangtse in 1942. But these were the only occasions on which toxic agents were used in World War II, although both sides carried gas masks and other protective measures. They had also stockpiled enormous quantities of chemical agents, presumably for use should the other side be the first to infringe the Geneva Protocol of 1925. Exactly what factors prevented a wider use of gas in World War II are not at all clear. What is clear, however, is that had toxic weapons been used the results would have been very different from those of World War I. The 1920s and 1930s were a time of very rapid scientific advance, particularly in physics and chemical technology. The first highly toxic insecticides were produced and these gave new clues to a class of toxic weapons totally unlike any that had been used in World War I.

It was, in fact, in the same year that the Italians were violating the Geneva Protocol that the next advance was made. Dr. Gerhard Schrader, working in Germany at the Leverkusen Laboratories of I. G. Farbenindustrie, was examining a class of organophosphorous chemicals in the hope of finding yet more toxic insecticides. The toxicity of one—later to be called tabun—was so high that its properties were pointed out to military personnel. Investigations then led to another compound named sarin and, much later in 1944, to a third called soman. These were the first nerve gases, much more toxic than even mustard gas and highly lethal in nature. Like mustard both the liquid on the skin and the vapor in the lungs produce severe effects. Two to four milligrams of sarin are thought to be lethal if inhaled in one breath. The most meaningful way of assessing the toxicity of such compounds is through their LCt_{50}—the concentration required to kill, on average, 50 percent of the population exposed to it for a certain length of time. The LCt_{50} for sarin is about 25 mg-min/m^3—which means that if 20 people inhale air which contains 25 milligrams of sarin in every cubic meter for one minute, 10 of them will die (these figures apply to active men—those breathing fast). Interpreting these figures again, one-tenth of an ounce of sarin dispersed in an aerosol in an average-size room would be sufficient to kill half the people who remained in the room for one minute breathing at a normal rate. Soman, the third compound to be developed, is even more toxic than sarin, and tabun is less so. Sarin is roughly 30 times as toxic as phosgene.

Unlike some other chemical agents, the nerve gases are general in their effects but act by interfering with one specific chemical involved in the mechanism by which nerves relax and contract muscles. When the brain passes a message through the body to operate a muscle such as the biceps, the message travels in electrical form along the nerves. When it reaches the junction or synapse between nerve and muscle a chemical known as acetylcholine is released. This chemical has one specific function: to initiate the sequence of events that leads to muscle contraction. The actual control over the muscle action is due to another chemical, an enzyme called cholinesterase. This breaks down the acetylcholine into its two constituent parts—acetic acid and choline—and so stops the muscle contraction.

The nerve gases inhibit the action of cholinesterase—they are therefore also known as anticholinesterases. As a result acetylcholine begins to build up in all the muscles. Most muscles in the body exist in complementary sets that pull in opposite directions, which is how one is able either to lift an arm up or return it to its former position (the arm can, of course, also drop back to position as a result of its weight but muscles are present to do the same job). The effect of the nerve gases, then, is to flood the muscles with acetylcholine, causing all the muscles—even those pulling in opposite directions—to try and contract. The result is that all coordinated action is lost and the muscles go into a state of fibrillation or vibration. This applies not only to the muscles of the arm and leg, for instance, but also to those that control excretion and respiration.

The nerve gases act very rapidly indeed. The first effects are somewhat similar to that of an irritant, or a chemical that affects the lungs. Vision becomes impaired, the chest feels tight and the nose begins to run. Quite quickly breathing becomes more difficult, the victim is sick and loses control over the muscles controlling excretion. The final stage of convulsion, caused by muscle fibrillation, leads to death by asphyxiation as control is lost of the respiratory muscles.

Nerve gases are both odorless and colorless. At room temperature they are liquids and can therefore be dispersed as an aerosol—a mist of very small droplets—which will vaporize quickly. Both the liquid and the gas are effective and will penetrate normal clothing—about 40 drops of liquid sarin deposited on the clothing of one soldier have a 50-50 chance of killing him. These chemicals are therefore difficult to detect and so have a dangerous surprise value. By the time the enemy has realized that a nerve gas attack has been made, he may well have received much more than a lethal dose.

As I have said, the nerve gases were discovered by the Germans in the 1930s. Tabun went into large scale production at Dyhernfurth, near Breslau, in April 1942. By the end of the war the Germans had stockpiled some 12,000 tons of tabun and had a production plant for sarin in standby condition which could produce 7,200 tons a year—roughly the equivalent of producing 100,000 tons of mustard. Could such a devastating weapon have altered the course of the war? If so, why did the Germans not make use of it?

These are difficult questions to answer. In his book *Tomorrow's Weapons,* Brigadier General J. H. Rothschild—who used to be in charge of research into chemical, biological, and radiological warfare for the U.S. Army Chemical Corps Research and Development Command— offers a number of reasons. Early in the war, of course, the Germans were having all the success they could reasonably hope for. They had already shown quite forcibly their total disregard for public opinion and international agreements, so these would probably not have been a strong inducement to refrain from the use of toxic agents. But, given the success of the early years of the war, they could have had just enough biting power to make the Germans think it might be wiser to have chemical weapons to fall back on should the war take a turn for the worse. The suggestion has also been made that, despite the sophistication of the conventional German war machine and the advanced stage that had been reached in the production of new chemical weapons, the German Army itself was not interested in chemical warfare and did not understand the principles of chemical action. Certainly little enough is known about the German administrative arrangements for implementing chemical warfare; there is a rumor, too, that Hitler ordered his commanders to use nerve gas to repel the D-Day invasion but that they refused to execute the command.

Rothschild also tells an intriguing story of scientific double bluff, which may well have had an effect on the Germans' decision. Throughout the war the Germans believed that the Allies had also discovered and stockpiled the nerve gases. This conclusion was partly based upon an extensive survey of the scientific literature which had revealed no mention of these chemicals. The Germans assumed that all reports on chemicals related to the nerve gases had been censored by the military because the Allies had already realized their importance. This being the case, the fear of retaliation—particularly during the later stages of the war when the Germans had most need of chemical weapons but when they would also have been most vulnerable—could well have played an important role in preventing the use of toxic agents.

Nothing in fact was further from the truth. As far as is known, no one outside Germany had discovered the nerve gases by 1939. The only new lethal chemical weapon that Britain and the United States had discovered, as late as 1941, was DFP (diisopropyl phosphorofluoridate). Although based on quite new principles, this was not a significant advance in terms of toxicity on the agents used during World War I and was regarded merely as a harassing agent. The other gases which the Allies still considered feasible at the outset of the Second World War were mustard gas, phosgene and, for certain special applications, hydrocyanic acid. These were not, of course, ever used with the exception of the Japanese mustard attacks.

During the war a large German plant for the manufacture of tabun was captured by the Russians and removed to the Soviet Union. The United States then began an active investigation of the organophosphorous compounds. Although tabun is easier to manufacture than sarin the latter is about four times as toxic; this was therefore adopted as the principal U.S. nerve gas. The Americans are now known to have large stockpiles of a number of nerve gases. In the United States tabun is known as GA, sarin as GB, and soman as GD. There is some mystery as to whether anything called GC exists and, if it does, what it is.

In the early 1950s British chemists discovered compounds related to the nerve gases but more toxic. They were investigated at Porton and by the Americans, who termed them the V agents (in particular VE and VX). Acting on similar principles to GA, GB, and GD, they differ mainly from the earlier nerve gases in that they are very much less volatile—which means, in effect, that they evaporate much more slowly. No specific information is available about their toxicity but Rothschild claims "a tiny droplet, if not removed immediately, will be absorbed (through the skin) and cause death." Contact with the skin is apparently painless and so the attack may go unnoticed until symptoms begin to appear. These agents are also very effective if inhaled as an aerosol. Like mustard gas, they remain a potential hazard for long periods of time because they evaporate so slowly. Spread over foliage they would represent a considerable danger to troops moving through a forest who were likely to brush against the leaves and so transfer a few drops to their clothing or skin. Equally, they could presumably be used with effect if spread onto the ground, in buildings, or on equipment, which had to be handled. Like the other nerve gases, inhalation produces severe effects almost immediately.

One of the most important results of the development of the V agents is that they once again broke the gas/gas mask deadlock. Their existence means that simple protection with a gas mask would be insufficient in the event of all-out chemical warfare. Through clothing and skin, they are far more toxic than mustard gas and soldiers or civilians attacked by a V agent would survive in the open only if they were completely covered in protective clothing.

There is no doubt at all that there have for some years been facilities in the United States for producing the nerve gases on a large scale, that these facilities have been used, and that stockpiles now exist of both the nerve gases themselves and of rockets, land mines, and artillery shells filled with nerve gas. GB has been produced at a plant known as the U.S. Rocky Mountain Arsenal at Denver, which in 1964 was in a standby condition but could be put back into service when required. GB or another nerve gas is produced at another plant in Newport, Indiana. With 300 civilian employees, the Indiana plant is known to have been in production for 24 hours a day for several years. This is the plant that produces gas-filled weapons and it is managed under contract by the "Food Machinery Corporation." According to the officer in charge of the plant, "from Newport, the rockets and artillery shells are shipped in normal army channels." The U.S. Army Field Manual FM 3-10 gives detailed instructions to field commanders for the tactical use of these weapons.

"These weapons" include the Corporal and the more advanced Sergeant missile. It is known that these were developed specifically to deliver a "chemical, biological, conventional or nuclear warhead." This information was made available a few years ago by the Guided Missile Department of the U.S. Army when details were released about the capabilities of the Sergeant missile. The state-

ment was in fact made contrary to defense policy; somehow it missed the normal security classification and was
given to journalists at a press conference. The Defense
Department later acknowledged that the statement was issued in error but no one has ever attempted to deny its
authenticity.

Sergeant is a highly versatile missile system capable
of delivering a 1,600 pound payload over a distance of 85
miles. A single missile of this kind liberating nerve gas in
aerosol form could produce at least a 33 percent casualty
rate over an area one mile in diameter. There is also evidence that the U.S. Army has developed much larger
chemical warheads for use with intercontinental ballistic
missiles, capable of a strike action several thousand miles
from the point of launching. In theory, a single bomber
carrying a similar payload of nerve gas could produce 30
percent casualties over an area of 100 square miles if the
population breathed the atmosphere unprotected for only
a few minutes. Whether or not this use of chemical weapons is likely is another matter and I shall return to it in
Chapter 8.

Clearly preparations have also been made for the deployment of chemical weapons on a small scale. In 1960
funds for the purchase of 11,300 M-55 rockets were made
available. This 115 millimeter rocket was developed specifically in the United States to deliver chemical warheads
over short ranges. They are fired from multiple launchers
containing 45 rockets and were designed after a German
rocket launcher originally developed to deliver tabun. The
U.S. Army also has mortars capable of firing chemical
warheads.

Of the air-to-ground delivery systems rather less is
known. The U.S. Air Force, according to Rothschild, has

1,000 pound cluster bombs that split up in the air into 76 smaller fragments whose descent is controlled by parachute so that the bomb does not bury itself in the ground. These are filled with GB. A variant on this theme is the bomb which comprises 264 smaller packages each of which acts as a small rocket when the main munition bursts in the air. On contact with the ground the contents of the bomb are scattered widely; bombs of this type have been used recently in Vietnam to deliver harassing agents such as tear gases and nausea-inducing compounds. The U.S. Navy also has its share of armaments. These include GB shells for 5-inch guns, GB-filled 5-inch rockets and GB-filled 500- and 750-pound bombs.

The Soviet Union has also taken great interest in the nerve gases. Because the Russians were able to capture and transport the German tabun (GA) plant during World War II, GA became their principal nerve gas. At least 50,000 tons had been stockpiled by the late 1950s and by now other, more toxic nerve gases have certainly been produced. In the U.S. report on *Chemical, Biological, and Radiological Warfare,* which I mentioned earlier, certain details of the Sino-Soviet chemical warfare machine were released. In 1959 their current military forces included more than 8 million men, grouped in more than 400 ground divisions. The Soviet Union could mobilize 300 additional divisions within 30 days or 500 divisions within a year. Each division has a chemical warfare unit associated with it and chemical troops are assigned to all echelons down to battalion level. In 1959 15 percent of Soviet military munitions were chemical and more than 50 Soviet factories were said to be capable of producing modern chemical warfare agents (the latter figure would, of course, be comparable to the number of factories in Western in-

dustrialized countries with the same capabilities). Furthermore, the decision to use Soviet chemical weapons is reputed to lie with military commanders.

The Soviet interest and awareness of chemical warfare
is also attested by reports of the activities of the civil defense organization known as DOSAAF. This organization
has set as its goal 20 hours of protective training against
chemical and biological weapons for the entire active
population.

It is clear, then, that the two major world powers are
committed to an expensive and active chemical warfare
program and that they also have production capabilities
available. There is every reason to believe that smaller
countries have just as intense an interest in these developments although their actual level of activity may currently
be a good deal lower. Chemical warfare is a cheap route to
massive offensive capability and so all the smaller but relatively advanced countries that anticipate military problems are certainly involved. Among these are countries
such as Egypt and Israel—the latter displaying its own
fear of possible chemical warfare during the 1967 war
when it received 20,000 gas masks ordered from West
Germany. Canada, France, and Sweden also maintain
powerful establishments, although the latter country is
openly concerned only with defense. China undoubtedly
has stockpiles of all the major post-World War II chemicals and has exported some of them to Egypt and to North
Vietnam.

In Britain two full-time establishments are maintained
at Porton Down near Salisbury—one concerned with
chemical warfare (the Chemical Defence Experimental
Establishment) and one with biological warfare (the
Microbiological Research Establishment). Both are officially concerned with defense only and at least some of

the scientists who work there do so strictly on that understanding. No weapons of any kind are manufactured in
bulk at Porton, although the harassing agent known as
CS was developed there in the early 1950s. As far as is
publicly known these are the only two units in the United
Kingdom with special responsibilities under the Ministry
of Defence for either chemical or biological warfare. A
firm in the south of England whose main products are concerned with minor munitions—Very pistol cartridges and
the like—also packages a number of tear gases as well as
CS. This chemical is exported abroad to a number of
countries.

What further activities are taking place in the United
Kingdom remains a mystery. There is no evidence of any
other form of manufacture of chemical agents or of operational stockpiles of them. The overall impression is that
Britain intends to abide by the Geneva Protocol (unless
she is first attacked in kind by an enemy), that she is working hard on defense matters and that no arrangements
have so far been made for the production of nerve gases.

The only record I know of the Western world's total
production capacity for toxic agents was given by the Soviet scientist, Academician M. M. Dubinin, at the 1959
Pugwash meeting (Pugwash is the international association of scientists dedicated to the preservation of world
peace). He put the figure at between 500,000 and 600,000
tons annually. Whether he was referring to all chemicals
of potential toxic use in war or just to all toxic materials
is not clear. But in any case—and as Dubinin himself pointed out—such estimates are bound to be misleading. The chemical technology required to produce toxic
compounds is common to both military and civilian technology and this is particularly true of the organophosphorous compounds. Structurally, the nerve gases are quite

similar to such common insecticides as parathion, systox, malathion, and others. If there ever were an urgent demand to produce nerve gases in quantity, civilian plants could be adapted to do it quickly and speedily. The worrying aspect of the current American production of nerve gas is simply that it is going on now. If required to, a number of other countries could do the same thing by exploiting civilian industry.

So far I have dealt only with the major chemicals used up to World War II and the development of the most toxic chemical weapons which have been standardized for military service—the nerve gases. But these do not represent the end of the search for toxic chemical weapons. Yet more toxic compounds are being sought and so are chemicals with what have euphemistically been called more "sophisticated" properties.

Readers may have noticed by now that many of the figures I have been discussing are dated to the late 1950s. This is no accident for it was during this period that the "whitewash" program for chemical and biological warfare was started in the United States. Information was deliberately leaked to arouse popular feeling that the United States should make a greater effort in this field. The true perspective on the situation was partially restored on October 1, 1959, when Walter Schneir wrote a penetrating article in *The Reporter* entitled "The campaign to make chemical warfare respectable" in which he exposed the real reason for this sudden release of new information.

This period at the end of the 1950s therefore represents a period of increased public awareness of chemical and biological warfare. There is a reason for this in that it also marks the end of a period concerned with what was essentially World War II chemical technology. It marks, in a sense, the end of the nerve gas period. One of the factors which led to the "whitewash" program was the realization by military thinkers that chemicals used in war do not necessarily have to produce either death or particularly painful symptoms. Indeed it was argued that one of the most valuable chemical weapons that could be produced would be a totally reversible one—one that left the victim entirely normal after a period of a few hours or perhaps even days. Ultimately it was this idea of "humane" chemical warfare that led to the unbuttoning of what was previously classified information; officials reasoned that if chemical warfare could be disguised under a humane barrier it might eventually gain greater public acceptance.

This was partly a trick to gain greater support for the development of new weapons. But it did also reflect a change in thinking about the aims of chemical warfare and a change in attitude towards its technology. The search for more and more powerful nerve gases had earlier been de-emphasized and instead several new research programs were begun to find new incapacitating agents. The research took two lines: one to find compounds which would affect the mind, the other to find compounds which would affect the body. One of the primary requirements of both programs was to discover chemicals that were completely reversible in their effect.

During the 1950s considerable attention was devoted to chemicals that would affect the mind. The idea was not that some science fiction effect could be obtained by drugs used to brainwash the enemy troops or civilians into different political convictions, but more simply that chemicals might be found which would temporarily upset the enemy's balance of reason. A search was therefore made among the hallucinogenic drugs of which by far the best known is lysergic acid (LSD). This chemical was originally isolated from ergot of rye and wheat in the form of *d-* lysergic acid diethylamide. In 1943 two Swiss chemists found a means of synthesizing it and from then on countless experiments have been made with it, with a great variety of social ends in view.

LSD is hallucinogenic: it disorients the mind, producing a whole range of effects which have much in common with the early stages of schizophrenia. Some scientists have claimed the effects include anxiety, depression, detachment, confusion, suspicion, and psychosis. Others claim they produce dramatic changes in personality leading to unprecedented peace, sanity, and happiness. Together with mescaline, derived from the peyote cactus, and psilocin and psilocybine, derived from a certain type of mushroom, these hallucinogenic drugs have earned conflicting descriptions as sacramental foods, devilish weapons, and wonder medicines (the latter from their use to cure a limited number of psychiatric cases). Undoubtedly they hold a great fascination for man which Dr. Timothy Leary and his colleagues have attempted to exploit as some kind of new religion. The basis of his claims for the hallucinogenic drugs are at least partly a series of experiments involving more than 300 subjects. Leary has reported that more than 91 percent of the Americans who took part in these experiments with what he calls "consciousness expanding" drugs reported pleasant, inspirational experiences. With only one ingestion of the drug, more than 60 percent of his subjects reported subsequent life changes for the better (such effects, of course, can hardly be described as reversible). All sorts of deductions have been made from these and similar experiments but only one need concern us here: Leary himself has said that such results indicate that these drugs have only limited military applications.

The battle for the mind is nothing new to the military arena. Even our word assassin comes originally from one of the first recorded uses of hallucinogenic drugs in war. Hashish was used extensively in the 16th and 17th centuries on Moslem troops in the hope that its effects would persuade them to go forth fearlessly to slay Christians. The warriors became known as hashshashin or hashish eaters—hence the word assassin. Whether or not this use of the drug was successful is another matter for hashish has a sedative as well as a hallucinogenic effect. But with the discovery of LSD new realms of psychological warfare were opened up because the drug was not sedative and because it was effective in minute amounts.

A chemical warfare agent which is to be effective must produce noticeable reactions at a dose of around 100 mg-min/m^3 or at dosages which correspond to 0.01 mg/kg of body weight—meaning that a man weighing 70 kg or about 160 pounds should respond to an injection into a vein of somewhat less than one thousandth of a gram. The only hallucinogenic drug widely known that falls easily into that category is LSD. About 70 micrograms inhaled produce severe results and between 100 and 1,000 times that dose are thought to be lethal. This means that 200 kilograms of the material spread to a depth of three meters would be sufficient to ensure that everyone within an area of half a square kilometer breathed in the effective oral dose within 15 seconds—in other words before he had time to put on a gas mask. If gas masks were not available, and the effective time could increase, as little as two kilograms might be effective.

These and other factors led military establishments in the United States in the 1950s to develop a hallucinogenic chemical agent which has been code named BZ. Its chemical composition has not been revealed. Its effects are said to be slowing of physical and mental activity, giddiness, disorientation, hallucination, and occasional maniacal behavior. It is delivered in the form of an aerosol and a film has been released showing the effect of this aerosol on a cat exposed to mice. Instead of chasing the mice, the cat became petrified with fear and made frantic efforts to escape from the cage, leaping several feet into the air every time a mouse ran near. The agent has also been tried experimentally on human troops; a guard affected by BZ tried to challenge an invading stranger at the gate house, forgot the password, and simply sat down on the ground in an apparent effort to puzzle the situation out. Furthermore, troops affected by BZ are said to be unaware that they are behaving in anything but a normal manner. The agent has been given field tests at the Dugway Proving Ground.

From what has been said, it should be apparent that such a specification hardly adds up to an ideal chemical weapon. One of the major problems is that it is impossible to predict what effects the hallucinogenic drugs will produce. It is quite conceivable that they will increase belligerency and yet at the same time make a man less effective in his duties. The aim of using such a weapon could hardly be to produce a belligerent, maniacal, and depressed machine-gun operator, or worse, Army commander with nuclear power at his elbow. Further, there is considerable doubt as to how reversible large doses of such drugs might be; certainly if the doses were really high, death could result and permanent psychological changes might be expected from slightly smaller doses.

Mainly for these reasons the research program in the United States in psychochemical weapons began to be deemphasized in the late 1950s and early 1960s. But at the same time officials continued to use the myth of truly reversible incapacitating weapons as a "humane umbrella," as E. James Liebermann has put it, "for even less justifiable pursuits." In other words, those responsible for policy in these fields used arguments that had already been at least partly rejected officially to secure greater public acceptance of the usefulness of humane chemical weapons, which would be entirely reversible. The idea that psychochemicals could play an important part in war was being publicly emphasized at the very time that official attention was wandering off into new directions.

One of the most important of these new directions was the search for an incapacitating agent that would act like an anesthetic. The Army Chemical Center at Edgewood Arsenal, in Maryland, is primarily responsible for the development of "anesthetic" agents within the United States. Although this program receives only a small percentage of the total chemical funds available, funding is not apparently the main problem. In an interview with *Missiles and Rockets* (October 5, 1964), Dr. Chalmers W. Sherwin, Deputy Director for Research and Technology of the Directorate for Research and Engineering, said: "We are having trouble finding people capable of working on this problem . . . What we require is not a large industrial productive effort but research and development in such fields as physiology, toxicology and microbiology." One of the difficulties of recruitment, he pointed out, was that "biologists who used to find it difficult to get a $5,000 grant are now being showered with funds as a result of the $1 billion National Institutes of Health programs and NASA's space biology programs." He added, "We are competing for the same people who are working, for example, on cancer research." Today the United States has clearly found one way of circumventing the problem of not being able to attract research workers to chemical and biological warfare research centers. It simply places contracts with scientists working at universities and colleges. This is the main reason why so many U.S. educational establishments are now engaged in chemical and biological warfare research.

Exactly what lines the next generation of chemical agents will take is not, of course, yet clear. Something is known of other chemicals which have been investigated, although they remain for the most part carefully guarded secrets. The most important trend to emerge from the search for new agents over recent years is another example of the ironic twists so common in this field: the aim is to borrow new knowledge from the pharmacologists in the hope of converting medically useful drugs into weapons of war. The establishments concerned have expressed interest in compounds which produce heat stroke, fainting, high blood pressure, muscular tremors, and nausea—the very side effects which drug houses spend so long on trying to eliminate. During 1962 about 400 possible drugs a month were supplied to the U.S. Army Chemical Center for further testing. As an example, many drug firms are producing muscle "relaxants" for the treatment of spastics and victims of rheumatoid arthritis. In 1959 the Director of Medical Research in the U.S. Army Chemical Warfare laboratories claimed that a compound had been found which in "minute" dosages produced an ascending spinal paralysis, which caused any victim to sink quickly on his haunches. This "knock down" compound was apparently reversible in its effects, the victim recovering completely within 24 hours.

Programs of this kind are still going on but BZ remains the only publicly known incapacitating drug which has been standardized. Meanwhile, of course, the search continues for more of the old-fashioned lethal chemicals which might eventually prove even more toxic than the latest nerve gases. One possible source is chemicals known as aryl carbamates, some 319 of which were examined for possible military use by the Allies in World War II. Many are as toxic as nerve gases and in 1952 the French reported a particularly complex one said to be ten times as toxic as one of the (unspecified) nerve gases.

Interest has also been taken in some of the naturally poisonous products produced by living organisms. The most important of these are probably sea-living animals such as the molluscs known as cones. These produce a toxin which has caused several natural fatalities in man. Contact with the tentacles of certain jellyfish is also lethal, as are the toxins produced by puffer fish and related animals. Like the nerve gases, many of the toxins produced by living organisms—especially the sea-living ones—produce paralysis of muscle tissue or block nerve conduction. This is not to say, of course, that any of these chemicals— or even synthetic ones, which resemble them, are ever likely to be used as weapons of war. At this stage we simply do not know. We do know, however, that military scientists in the United States and elsewhere are at least aware of these possibilities and have investigated them. They have published, for instance, a lengthy list of the so-called by-products of research into chemical and biological warfare, which are used as evidence that such research programs benefit not only the military security of the nation but also produce peaceful applications. An example from the 1959 report to the U.S. House of Representatives illustrates both the peaceful applications and the military intent that lies behind them: "The paralytic poisoning in man often caused by eating toxic clams and mussels was isolated in relatively pure form from clam and mussel tissues by the Chemistry Branch at Fort Detrick in collaboration with Canadian associates in 1954. The isolation of this product in purified form has been of great value to the U.S. Public Health Service, Food and Drug Administration, and commercial shellfish interests. The purified poison is now used internationally as a standard for the bioassay for the poison in shellfish products. Previous to the isolation of the purified poison, no reference standard was available and considerable difficulty arose mainly from the fact that the bioassay was interpreted differently in each country and even in different laboratories in the same country."

If this book had been written two years ago, we would by now have reached the end of the chapter on chemical agents. Unhappily there are now two other uses of chemical warfare that have to be mentioned. The first concerns the use of chemicals by the Egyptians in the Yemen. Repeated attacks were made during 1966 and 1967 and several hundred casualties were produced, many of them eventually proving fatal. The International Red Cross was called in to investigate. The claims were substantiated, and it was found that both mustard gas and phosgene had been used. Critics suggested the Egyptians were "practicing" for their obviously impending war against Israel. But in the event the Israeli air attack proved so effective in June 1967 that the Egyptians had little chance to show whether or not they intended using chemical weapons. But it was later reported that dumps of Egyptian chemicals were found abandoned in the Sinai desert.

Earlier, in 1965, the Americans began to use incapacitating chemicals in Vietnam. The gases were all of the tear or nausea producing variety, which—as was hastily pointed out by Defense officials—are of the type used in civilian riot control. The British police have used similar compounds more than 120 times in the past five years in overseas bases.

The gases used in Vietnam—described by Defense officials as "benevolent incapacitators"—produce only a temporary effect. They include a chemical code-named DM (which used to be called Adamsite) that has been used in ton quantities and which was described by Robert McNamara, the U.S. Defense Secretary, as a "pepper-like irritant that affects the eyes and mucous membranes, and causes sneezing, coughing, headache, tightness in the chest, nausea and vomiting." It incapacitates for between half an hour and an hour. The other two chemicals used are known as CN and CS. The first is a lacrimatory agent, which also irritates the upper respiratory passages and the skin. Its effects last only three minutes. CS was developed in the early 1950s at the CDEE in Porton and causes chest pains as well as producing more severe irritation than CN. It is effective for between five and ten minutes. All three compounds are sold by a number of companies in the United States, packaged into cartridges, grenades, and squirting devices, and CS is manufactured in the United States under British license.

According to press reports the Vietcong retaliated in kind within the year and American troops are reported to have captured an ammunition dump containing chemical agents of the incapacitating variety. As a leader in the *New Scientist* (September 29, 1966) put it: "The Vietnam war is being waged with all the nonnuclear ferocity to which weapons technology can aspire. In that unhappy country chemical agents are being used on a scale unknown since the First World War." The leader was referring principally to the use of chemical agents to destroy crops and also to strip the foliage off trees and thus remove the cover in which troops may be hiding. These are applications which I shall discuss more fully in Chapter 7 and they are not the applications to which the world at large reacted so strongly. But the news that the Americans were using gas against Vietcong troops produced a storm of protest.

There were in fact three quite different kinds of reaction to the news. Headlines such as "Poison Gas—An Arsenal of Horror Waits in the Wings" typify one of them. On the other hand, *Industrial Research,* an American semipopular controlled circulation magazine, wrote: "An intelligent citizenry should be neither shocked nor chagrined to learn that the United States is so deeply committed to the development of toxic weaponry." The article concerned leaped to the defense of the American action and called for a rational approach to the situation which, it claimed, had become "smothered in a smog of emotion." The third kind of reaction was typified by the petition sent to the U.S. President by leading scientists and which is quoted in full in Chapter 10. These three different reactions need to be examined in more detail if they are to be intelligently assessed.

Public sympathy undoubtedly lies with the first—particularly for those who have memories of gas warfare in World War I. To them—and to many more who have a far less clear idea of what chemical warfare involves—an "arsenal of horror" is perhaps not an inept description for the stockpiles of chemical weapons possessed by most major nations. Whether these opinions can really be said to be informed ones is another matter. Compared with conventional weapons, incapacitating chemicals, it can be argued with some justification, are more humane. The Americans claimed that their use of gas in Vietnam did a job that needed to be done with less wounding and less

loss of life than would otherwise have been the case. They
were probably right.

But this justification for the use of chemicals in Vietnam is an extremely short-term one; it does not take into
account the deeper issues involved or the chemical escalation to which it might lead. The "reasoned approach" of
the article in *Industrial Research*—which is closely aligned
with official policy in the United States—is also shallow.
It limits itself to one specific application of chemical warfare without regard for any of the wider and more profound issues involved. These were aptly summarized in the
petition sent to President Johnson. There is no clear dividing line between incapacitating and lethal chemical weapons and there is no clear dividing line between chemical
and biological weapons. They merge as insidiously into
one another as gunpowder did into TNT or the first atomic
pile in Chicago did into the hydrogen bomb. The real cause
for alarm at the Vietnam action is not that the chemicals
being used are inhumane; it is that for the first time
since 1918 chemical weapons are again being used on a
massive scale. Such an action is not likely to lead to a
more congenial atmosphere at the disarmament table.
But it is likely to lead to the use of progressively more
lethal chemical agents, just as did the French use of tear
gas early in World War I. But there is a difference; this
time the escalation could continue through the chemical
agents and on to the biological ones, which have never before been used.

CHAPTER 4

When Half the World Was Ill

Ring-a-ring o' roses,
A pocketful of posies,
A-tishoo, a-tishoo,
We all fall down.

Nursery rhyme commenting on 14th-century plague

THE WORST disaster that has ever befallen mankind was not either of the world wars or even the invention of nuclear weapons. It was, in fact, a pandemic of disease that swept Europe some 600 years ago: the Black Death of 1348-50. In those three years plague killed more than a quarter of the population of Europe and produced an economic decline from which it took more than a century to recover.

A pandemic is simply another word for an epidemic of such proportions that it sweeps across a whole country or even continent. Epidemics of this size—and particularly those of plague—have somehow become loosely associated with the probable effects of biological warfare. Plague certainly is one of the diseases which nations have considered as a possible biological weapon but it is not by any means the only one. Nor has serious military consideration been given to producing an outbreak of disease of anything like the magnitude of the Black Death. Not the least of the problems to be considered in biological warfare is selecting those biological weapons that are likely to produce their effect only in a target area of limited size. This is a serious problem for, as the major pandemics of the past show, some diseases are quite capable of establishing themselves on a continental or even global scale.

Because disease has had such a profound effect on social evolution it is, in principle, a powerful weapon with which to control not only men's bodies but also their minds. Probably it would be the supreme weapon were it not for the mercifully numerous difficulties that surround any attempt to produce disease artificially. Fortunately we have acquired the medical skills with which to limit outbreaks of infectious disease long before we have learnt how to spread disease with anything like the efficiency of the natural mechanisms which operated until the early part of this century. Any nation that now tries to spread disease deliberately has two difficult problems with which to contend. First, to develop methods capable of producing outbreaks as serious as those which used to occur naturally. And, second, to maintain the efficiency of these methods in the face of modern medical knowledge and practice. What then are the diseases that represent potential threats in the event of biological warfare?

Plague is caused by a bacterium, *Pasteurella pestis,* which is transmitted via fleas from about 200 different kinds of rodent—the most famous being the black rat. The disease itself occurs in three forms which are recorded in the nursery rhyme quoted at the beginning of this chapter. Pneumonic plague affects primarily the lungs ("A-ti-shoo, a-tishoo") and is caused by the bacteria being inhaled. Bubonic plague is probably the form of the disease with which most people associate it. It produces a red rash ("Ring-a-ring o' roses") and swellings of the lymph glands, which used to be called buboes; if the disease takes its most extreme and agonizing course, these eventually burst. Septicemic plague is caused by the bacteria attacking the bloodstream and it produces dark discolorations of the skin after which the Black Death was named. Untreated, all three forms are normally fatal within less than a week; septicemic plague can be fatal within 24 hours ("We all fall down").

According to William L. Langer, Professor of History at Harvard University, the Black Death originated in the ports of Italy presumably because plague-infested rats were transported there by merchant ships coming from the Black Sea. This was early in 1348. By June of that year it had reached Hungary, northern France, and almost as far as Madrid. Six months later it covered the south of England and within another year had spread into Scotland, Scandinavia, and Poland. By the end of 1350 it blanketed more or less the whole of Europe. Florence lost half its population, Hamburg two-thirds, and the population in England fell from 3.8 million in 1348 to 2.1 million in 1374. Western and central Europe as a whole took nearly two centuries to regain the 1348 level of population.

No one, of course, understood the cause or origins of the disease. Doubtless this contributed to the widespread panic that ensued and which itself contributed to the spreading of disease. Although drastic measures were taken to isolate those already afflicted, nearly everyone who could afford to do so fled their towns and villages as soon as the first victims in it were taken ill. They must certainly have carried with them the plague bacillus, almost certainly plague-infected fleas, and probably plague-infected rats as well. Those that remained indulged themselves in what Samuel Pepys described as "lewd and dissolute behaviour," mimicking the behavior of the Greeks 1,700 years previously whose reactions to the plague in Athens were described in very similar terms by Thucydides. In short, one half of the population fled, the other half, thinking their lifetime had suddenly been curtailed—as indeed it was about to be—made the most of their remaining weeks in drunkenness, orgies, crime, and violence. As Boccaccio wrote, "the reverend authority of the laws, both human and divine, was all in a manner dissolved and fallen into decay. . . ."

Such a reaction is not necessarily typical of human disaster. When one remembers the way Londoners responded to sustained bombing during the blitz in the last war, or the way mining towns recover from disasters that sometimes take a toll of human life almost as high, one realizes that other factors must have been operating during the plague, apart from the size of the disaster. One must certainly have been fear of the unknown. The Black Death was still more than 500 years from the era of scientific medicine and no one understood the nature of disease or its causes. Another was that disease was probably the single most feared catastrophe that could occur. In the 14th century life expectancy was short and most people died from disease in any case. The people knew its killing power far better than we do today. They would realize only too well that the chance of surviving a pandemic such as the Black Death was not large. Eighty percent of those that contracted the disease died. And in 14th-century Europe more than 30 million people did contract it.

Once the plague had a grip on Europe it did not let go easily. There were recurrent outbreaks up to the 16th century and another major epidemic, the Great Plague of 1664, in the following century. Thereafter, however, the disease died down, although it has always been present to some degree in Africa and Asia. An outbreak in the United States in 1919 killed 13 out of 14 people and 34 out of 41 died in an outbreak in 1924. During the period 1900-1966 no more than 111 known cases of bubonic plague were reported in the United States, although there are now signs that the disease is again on the increase. American public health officials are worried on two counts.

The first is that although rodents such as the black rat are the common carriers of the disease other animals—including such domestic ones as rabbits and chipmunks—can also carry it. Such animals are a good deal more lovable than the rat and this encourages closer contact with humans. A plague-infested animal of this kind in one of the American recreational parks could provide a focus of infection that has a good chance of spreading more widely. The second factor which may be aiding the spread of plague is the great increase in air cargo flights—which may carry plague-infested rats just as ships did in an earlier age—combined with increasing urbanization. Such developments give the urban rat maximum chance of picking up infection from wild rats and then spreading it in slum areas within a city where conditions are often sufficiently insanitary for both the rat and its fleas to breed. In 1966 both Mexico and Arizona recorded cases of plague in hunters returning from open country. Providing the infection remains in unpopulated land, there is little chance of the disease spreading. But if the infection is transmitted from country vectors to city ones the problem is much more severe. Plague is now known to exist in a wide area of the United States extending from California as far east as Oklahoma.

There has also been a recent outbreak of plague in Vietnam. Between January 1 and August 5, 1966, 2,002 cases were reported of which 116 died. North of Saigon

22 out of 29 provinces were affected in late 1966 whereas five years previously only one province was affected. More than half the world's reported deaths from plague in 1966 occurred in Vietnam, where wartime conditions are, of course, ideal for both the animal vectors—rodents and fleas—to multiply.

The flea that is most widely known as a plague carrier is *Zenopsylla cheopis*. It spreads the disease to its human host either because it carries bacteria in its mouth or because the flea itself becomes infected. When this happens the flea's stomach may become completely blocked and the blood it sucks unable to enter. The blood is therefore returned to its human host contaminated with bacteria. This is not, however, the only means by which plague can be spread. If the lungs of a plague victim become heavily infected, bacteria may be exhaled and become airborne. They may then be inhaled producing pneumonic plague in another host. In this way the disease can be transmitted man to man. If plague is ever used as a biological weapon, it will almost certainly be transmitted as pneumonic plague; the bacteria will be spread as an aerosol spray just as are chemical herbicides and insecticides.

I have dealt at some length with plague because it is the first disease with which most people associate biological warfare. It is also a disease that has had a profound effect on the history of mankind and which has occurred several times in pandemic proportions. It is not, however, by any means the only disease that has been considered in biological warfare. Altogether about 160 different infectious diseases are known. These are the illnesses produced by a variety of different microorganisms or germs as distinct from complaints which result from the gradual deterioration of human tissue. The organisms that cause infectious disease have been studied in great detail over the past hundred years and there is no longer any great mystery about the ways in which they spread. Plague itself, as I have said, is caused by a bacterium. So are many of the other common diseases which are familiar now mainly as those complaints for which the doctor prescribes antibiotics. They include tuberculosis, cholera, and even such apparently innocuous infections as boils and abscesses.

Bacteria are officially classified as a form of plant life. They are, of course, a very specialized variety, notably in that they are single-celled organisms. The smallest are only about one ten-thousandth of an inch across and in that tiny volume is contained all the equipment needed for life—chemical factories, energy storehouses, information banks, and many other cell components. The whole is encased in a relatively tough cell wall through which the foods needed by the bacterium diffuse. Inside the cell the organism turns these simple chemicals into more complex ones; this is the process known as metabolism. The chemical products which bacteria produce are primarily responsible for the diseases they cause. The chemicals interfere with the normal metabolism of the human body producing such secondary results as a high fever and high temperature which we recognize as symptoms of the disease.

These effects are accentuated by the efforts the body must make to destroy the invading bacteria. These organisms reproduce, quite simply, by splitting in two. They may do so either slowly or very quickly—some bacteria are capable of dividing every few minutes. If a single bacterium is capable of dividing every half hour, and none of the offspring die off, the bacterial population will increase with enormous speed. In less than 12 hours it will produce more than a million individuals. To prevent this happening, the body must mobilize its attacking forces with equal rapidity.

The body cells capable of attacking bacteria and other organisms which are foreign to the body are known as immunocytes. When they come into contact with bacteria, they not only recognize the bacteria as foreign material but also produce substances known as antibodies that either kill or inactivate the bacteria. This feat is made even more remarkable by the fact that the type of antibody produced is specific to the type of bacteria invading the body. The whole process—known as the immunological reaction—is an extremely complicated one and is still far from being completely understood. It involves several different types of specialized cells, each capable of producing several thousand types of antibody, as well as yet other types of cell responsible for clearing away the debris of inactivated bacteria. But the battle between antibodies and bacteria is never a foregone conclusion; complicated though the defense system may be, it is often beaten by the invading bacteria with the result that serious infection and even death follow.

There are two principal means of helping the body wage its battle against bacteria. The first consists of introducing into the blood stream chemicals that are capable of destroying bacteria. Since World War II penicillin, streptomycin, and a host of other antibiotics have enormously reduced the mortality of bacterial disease. These antibiotics work in a number of different ways—typically by attacking the bacterial cell wall or by interfering radically with the chemical processes that go on inside the cell. Most of them, however, are specific in their action, attacking only a single species of bacteria or a group of related ones. This is important for there are still some bacterial diseases that cannot be treated at all, or only rather ineffectively, with antibiotics. From the point of view of biological warfare, cholera is probably the most important of these. Another is a very rare disease known as melioidosis, which produces fever and usually death; only a few hundred cases have ever been recorded, although it has recently broken out in Vietnam. Of 32 U.S. soldiers who had contracted it by February 1967 nine had died.

It is also possible to vaccinate against bacterial disease and protect a population, or a percentage of it, from any future outbreaks of the disease. The purpose of vaccination is to stimulate the body into producing antibodies against the particular organisms concerned before they actually cause disease. One way is to inject a small quantity of the organism responsible for a related but much milder form of the disease. The first recorded uses of "vaccination," in which patients were infected with the relatively harmless cowpox to protect them against the much more serious smallpox, where carried out in this way. Alternatively, it is possible to inject into the blood stream dead organisms which, though they cannot produce disease, can still stimulate the production of antibodies.

Two of the most important diseases as regards biological warfare against man—as distinct from animals—are plague and cholera. Cholera has been known, at least in a mild form, since the beginnings of history. It produces nausea, vomiting, diarrhea, painful stomach cramps and it is sometimes or often fatal. Curiously it appears to have remained relatively dormant for most of human history, the first major recorded epidemic being in 1816-23 when it spread to Southeast Asia, China, Japan, parts of Africa, and the eastern shore of the Mediterranean. Another outbreak occurred in 1826-37 and this time it reached America and most of Europe. In 1830 cholera reached Moscow and 60,000 people fled the city; in 1832, more than 50,000 fled from New York for the same reason. In six months in Leeds in the same year there were 700 deaths from cholera and a Dr. Robert Baker made a study of its geographical incidence. He concluded the disease was particularly common in the crowded and insanitary conditions that prevailed in slum areas. From then on, the hunt to find the cause of the disease quickened and in 1848 came the classic work of Dr. John Snow in Soho. In this very small area of London there occurred 500 cholera deaths in a space of ten days. Snow's investigations established the outbreak started on the night of August 31-September 1 and, although three-quarters of the population fled the area within the week, Snow was able to locate the addresses of the victims and to plot them on a map. He found they clustered in a remarkable way round a street pump from which the local inhabitants drew their water. At Snow's request the handle of the pump was removed and the outbreak died almost over night. Snow had proved that cholera was caused by contaminated water.

Although his findings took some time to catch on, they were one of the most important spurs towards the establishment of standards of public health and the essential step of water purification. These measures helped reduce the spread of the disease but the real breakthrough came later in the nineteenth century with the discovery of the organism that caused cholera. Under the microscope it appeared to have the shape of a comma and, unlike normal bacteria, it vibrated violently to and fro when in its active state. It was therefore called *Vibrio comma*. Once this discovery was made, the way was clear to the development of anticholera vaccines, first from live material and later from killed organisms. They are remarkably effective although to this day their effects are short-lived; cholera vaccinations should be renewed about every six months.

While these discoveries were going on, the disease appeared anyway to have passed its peak. The last outbreak in the Western Hemisphere occurred in 1911 and in Europe in 1923. But cholera is still a disease that must be treated with great respect as was shown dramatically in Egypt in 1947. In that year merchants gathered for the annual date fair in El Korein on the Nile Delta. Nearby was a construction site on which 6,000 laborers were working. Cholera, from an unknown source, broke out in the town and began to spread. General panic ensued and the merchants and laborers fled. But instead of avoiding the disease they carried it with them to all parts of Egypt. Before long 33,000 cases had developed and concern became worldwide—partly because previous outbreaks had been documented with clarity and partly because most of the world had long been free from the disease. Altogether 20 million doses of the vaccine were flown to Egypt, each dose containing some 8 million dead organisms. The epidemic was halted but not for four months or before there had been 20,000 deaths from cholera.

This is a salutary tale for it occurred only 20 years ago and not during wartime (when insanitary conditions always favor outbreaks of disease). Since then the treatment of cholera has improved but not spectacularly. The disease is still prevalent in Southeast Asia where it causes some 6,000 deaths a year and infects about 20,000 people. Immunity to the disease in other parts of the world is limited, largely because the vaccine's effects are short-lived and because the disease has not been known there for some 50 years. If cholera could be introduced anywhere where it is not now endemic, it could spread swiftly and might require a massive vaccination program to eradicate it. But unless standards of public hygiene in the Western world were first very much reduced it would have little chance of spreading through contaminated water or food supplies in the way that it did in the 19th-century epidemics.

Before moving on to the next group of disease-producing organisms, I should perhaps mention three other bacterial diseases of possible wartime significance. They are all primarily diseases of domestic animals but they can also be transmitted to man. They represent at least a potential threat to both livestock and to man himself. The first, glanders, is an acute respiratory infection, against which there is no satisfactory vaccine, although it can be treated with antibiotics. The second is known as brucellosis and occurs in cattle, producing abortion (the causative organisms are *Brucella abortus* and two related species). It can be transferred to man either directly or through the drinking of contaminated milk. In man, its mortality rate is only in the neighborhood of a few percent but it is an incapacitating disease which can last for months. The symptoms are complex and difficult to diagnose—one authority has associated the disease with no less than 230 different symptoms. Although it has been completely eradicated in several countries, including Scandinavia, it is still prevalent in the United Kingdom. Indeed, estimates suggest that one quarter of the dairy herds are infected with the organisms involved and that 2 percent of them produce contaminated milk. The current incidence of the disease in man is not known but there are probably one or two thousand cases of it every year in the United Kingdom.

The third disease, anthrax, is possibly of even greater relevance to biological warfare. It is caused by the bacterium *Bacillus anthracis*. Unlike nearly all the other bacteria of direct relevance to biological warfare, this bacterium is capable of forming extremely hardy spores which can survive in soil for years and can even live in boiling water for several minutes. When in the spore form, the bacterium is totally inactive and begins to reproduce only when it reverts to the normal vegetative form in which bacteria normally exist. This was the bacterium which officials from Britain's Microbiological Research Establishment at Porton sprayed on the island of Gruinard in Scotland during the last war. Since then access to the island has been forbidden to the public but it is revisited yearly to see if the danger of infection has passed. So far it has not, and officials have stated that it might be another hundred years before all signs of anthrax have disappeared from the soil. Such is the surviving power of the anthrax spore.

Thanks to antibiotics, the bacterial diseases, as I have said, are no longer the killers they once were. There is, however, another equally large group of diseases produced by a totally different kind of organism: the virus. These microorganisms are even smaller than bacteria, some measuring less than one millionth of an inch in diameter. They are also quite different in that they cannot strictly be said to be living organisms. A virus on its own requires no food, is unable to reproduce itself, and exists simply as a rather complex piece of organic chemistry. The center of a virus consists of nucleic acid and this is the infective portion. The nucleic acid is surrounded by a protective protein coat. When a virus becomes absorbed by the body—usually through the lungs—it will enter one of the cells of its host. There the nucleic acid it contains will upset the normal chemical functioning of the cell. Instead of producing the proteins which it normally does, the cell will be made, by the viral nucleic acid, to produce the proteins that make up the coat of the virus. While this is going on the nucleic acid itself will duplicate using chemicals already available in the cell to do so. In this way further virus is formed, which can, in turn, infect another cell

and reproduce itself yet again. Against such organisms
antibiotics are relatively useless. They are designed to interfere specifically with the metabolism of a whole cell—
the bacterium. Viruses are very much smaller than a cell
and they possess no metabolism to be interfered with.
There is still no real cure for viral diseases, although vaccines generally work better against viral disease than
against bacterial ones.

The best known of all the viral diseases is the common
cold. There is still no real cure for this and so many viruses
are involved that it is even proving extremely difficult to
produce an effective vaccine against it. It is not a disease,
however, which even in its most virulent form is likely to
be considered as a biological weapon. Influenza is
a slightly more serious possibility even though its effects
are not normally very severe. In its time it has produced pandemics of almost staggering proportion. The
largest was probably that of 1918 and 1919. This was
caused, it was later discovered, by what would normally
have been a relatively harmless influenza virus. But what
made its effects so severe was that it was coupled with the
spread of what normally would also have been a relatively
harmless bacterium, which can be found, quite naturally
in about 10 percent of pigs—and, for that matter, humans.
Together these microorganisms spread across almost the
entire world causing not just simple influenza but also conditions that led to pneumonia—the disease which was
ultimately to cause so many deaths. Conservative estimates suggest that more than 20 million died in that pandemic and that 500 million—at that time a third of the
world population—were afflicted by it at one time or another. In statistical terms, then, it spread to far more people
than did the Black Death; the mortality rate, however, was
very much lower at 4 rather than 80 percent.

The public reactions it produced were not, of course, anything like as alarming as those which accompanied the Black Death. In the United States the pandemic occurred towards the end of World War I and newspapers devoted relatively little space to it, although it accounted for one quarter of the total deaths sustained by the American military forces throughout the war. The Germans claimed that American bodies were being piled high in the streets of New York—a gross exaggeration which many states took good care to make sure could not happen. San Francisco made it illegal to appear in public not wearing a face gauze and New York City imposed a fine on anyone found spitting on the pavement. The word began to get around that the disease had been deliberately spread by the Germans and it became known as the German plague. This idea was, of course, quite without foundation and the government was quick to deny it. But this pandemic does lend vivid illustration to the difficulties which any country might encounter if it tried to foster the spread of disease. If the disease had been spread by the Germans they might well have counted the operation a military success on account of the effect it had on the Americans. But they might not have reckoned on the disease becoming a worldwide pandemic; and they certainly would not have anticipated that more than half the deaths it caused—more than 10 million—occurred in one country: India. This was the greatest death toll which even a land as stricken with disease as India was, and is, had ever encountered within the space of a few months.

It would be easy to continue this chapter almost indefinitely with accounts of the major pandemics of the past. I will confine myself, however, to only two more— smallpox and yellow fever. Both these are worth considering in a little more detail because they have produced important epidemics in the past and because, if any viral diseases are ever used in biological warfare, they are among the possible contenders.

Smallpox is said to have been brought to Europe by returning crusaders. In any event it rapidly became one of Europe's most feared diseases. More than 90 percent of the Europeans who survived into adulthood in the 18th century are said to have had smallpox and more than one person in ten died from it. In the Old World the disease seems to have been so prevalent that outbreaks were often not recorded at all—and never so systematically as were the isolated but severe outbreaks of less common diseases such as plague. When smallpox reached the New World, however, the effect was catastrophic for the disease had not previously been known there and the indigenous inhabitants had no protection or immunity against it. Between 1517 and 1530 the disease is said to have caused the deaths of two million American Indians. The ferocious way in which it spread can be explained at least partly by the fact that smallpox is one of the most contagious of all infectious diseases. According to Professor J. F. D. Shrewsbury it was really smallpox and not Cortez that won Mexico for Spain. Within six months of its introduction among the Aztecs it had killed 3½ million people—more than half the total population of the Aztec Empire and in his book *Illustrations of the manners, customs and condition of the North American Indians,* G. Catlin wrote in 1876: "Thirty millions of white men are now struggling and scuffling for the goods and luxuries of life over the bones and ashes of twelve millions of red men, six millions of whom have fallen victims to the smallpox, the remainder to the sword, the bayonet, or whisky." As I have mentioned, one of the first documented cases of the use of biological warfare involved the donation of smallpox-infected materials to Indian chiefs by the colonists to help spread the disease among their people. How successful this maneuver was is not recorded, for accidental infection from the white man was already taking such a savage toll of the Indian population.

Smallpox is no longer the fearsome disease it once was for extremely effective vaccines against it have been available since the last century. These have virtually eliminated the disease in many countries—including the United Kingdom and the United States—with the result that vaccination has become much more lax in these countries. The disease is still prevalent in other parts of the world—notably certain areas of Asia—and visitors are not normally admitted from these areas to other countries unless in possession of a valid smallpox vaccination certificate. This has perhaps lured other populations into a false feeling of security for it is estimated that only half the population of the United Kingdom and the United States has been vaccinated against the disease. If it did gain substantial entry into one of these countries, it might produce a serious epidemic. For this reason it must still be included among the possible biological weapons, even though effective vaccines are available.

Yellow fever is a viral disease which is today endemic in large areas of northern South America and in central Africa. Monkeys and other wild animals act as a reservoir of the disease, which is spread to humans by a mosquito, mainly *Aedes aegypti*. It seems that the disease has been known for a long time in Africa but that it did not spread to human populations in the Americas until it was first carried there by African slaves. During the early colonization of the West Indies it took a terrible toll of life, particularly among white men who seemed less well protected against it than either the Africans or the local populations.

The disease is better known, however, for the part it played in delaying the construction of the Panama Canal. Fresh from his triumph over the Suez Canal, the Frenchman Ferdinand de Lesseps turned his attention, in 1876, to the construction of a similar canal across the American isthmus. His work force was so completely devastated by yellow fever that the attempt had later to be abandoned completely, although £64 million were spent on the abortive project. But by 1901 Surgeon-General Gorgas had successfully identified the cause of the disease as the bite of the mosquito. The mosquito was eradicated from the area and in 1904 the United States successfully took over the job of building the canal. By the time it was open in 1914 there had been no further cases of yellow fever in the area for some time.

Though effective, eliminating the infective mosquitoes could not be considered as a final answer to the yellow fever problem. Indeed, with the construction of the Panama Canal, the Rockefeller Foundation saw a new danger that improved traffic between the New and Old Worlds might bring: transportation of the yellow fever virus from Africa or America to the Far East where it had thus far never appeared. The consequences of this might indeed have been devastating and accordingly the Foundation spent $14 million between 1916 and 1949 in an effort to eliminate the disease from the face of the world.

Their work was largely successful because, more or less at the same time that it was found that the fever was transmitted by mosquitoes, scientific work of even more fundamental importance was going on. In 1898 the Dutch botanist Beijerinck had proved once and for all that all disease is not caused by "germs." He found that a liquid passed through a filter fine enough to strain out even the smallest bacteria would still cause disease if it was afterwards rubbed on the stems of tobacco plants. He called his discovery virus but believed that it was essentially a "living contagious fluid." Just three years after the discovery of the first plant virus came the discovery of the first virus to cause human disease—the yellow fever virus. But although it was the first to be discovered, this virus has still not been purified and crystallized. Indeed, it was to be many years before the viral nature of yellow fever was accepted by scientists.

It was not till 1934 that the French Government first attempted to develop a human yellow fever vaccine on a large scale. Combining it with a smallpox vaccine they started a huge campaign in Africa, vaccinating 56 million people between 1939 and 1953. Yellow fever virtually disappeared from the regions in which the vaccine was used. But although effective, this vaccine did sometimes have serious side effects and new efforts were made to find an improved vaccine.

The yellow fever virus is one of the smallest known. So far it has never even been observed in the electron microscope. Further, it is one of the most labile—it is easily killed by heat and, curiously, by salt water. For some reason, too, the killed virus is incapable of stimulating the production of antibodies; there is therefore no prospect at present of being able to produce a killed vaccine from it.

A team of scientists in the United States began to investigate the possibility of growing yellow fever virus on tissue culture. Viruses, as I have explained, cannot reproduce themselves unless they are in a living animal or plant cell. They cannot therefore be grown like bacteria on a bed of nutrient fluid. But they can be grown in living cells, which are themselves kept alive in a nutrient medium. These cultures can be kept going indefinitely if certain types of cells are used; one of the most important types is embryo material. Accordingly, Dr. Max Theiler and his colleagues grew a particularly virulent strain of the yellow fever virus on chick embryo material. They kept viruses and cells reproducing for more than three years without passing the virus back to an animal host. During this time they constantly altered the conditions in which the tissue cultures were grown and the kind of embryo material on which they grew the virus. And during the winter of 1935-36 a remarkable event occurred; the virus underwent a mutation—a change in genetic properties—which rendered it much less virulent. Indeed when Theiler tested his mutant virus on animals he found its effects were far from severe; his mutant bore much the same kind of relationship to yellow fever as cowpox does to smallpox. He had found a material from which a completely safe and effective vaccine could be made. This is now in standard use in all parts of the world where yellow fever threatens with the exception of Africa. The vaccine lasts for at least six years and it is one of the best vaccines known to science. Today, more than 10 million people have been vaccinated against yellow fever.

Epidemic diseases, as we have seen, can be spread throughout a population or part of it in a number of different ways. Some, such as plague and yellow fever, are spread by animal vectors—in these cases mainly the flea and the mosquito. And even if the disease is eliminated from a population, a reservoir of infection still exists; the plague reservoir is carried by rats, the yellow fever one by monkeys. But these diseases are not spread in the same way as the common cold or flu—they are not contagious and (with one important exception) are spread directly from man to man only rarely. They are caused mainly by the bites of fleas and mosquitoes during which the causative organisms are injected into the blood stream. The transmission of plague, as I mentioned earlier, is more complicated because it occurs in three forms and one of these—pneumonic plague—can be passed directly from man to man; the plague bacilli can be inhaled in large enough doses to initiate infection. But an epidemic of a vector-transmitted disease is not usually caused because people pass it from one individual to the next but because, for some reason, they become more exposed to the bites of infected vectors. This may be because the vectors themselves have suddenly become much more numerous or, as happens with plague, because the rats the fleas normally feed on are in short supply and so turn their unwanted attention to humans.

There are other diseases, such as cholera, which are transmitted neither by vectors nor by inhalation. These are the diseases that are usually produced by the ingestion of contaminated food or drink. They can also be transferred from man to man directly because the microorganisms that cause the disease are often excreted. If they can find their way back into drinking water or food supplies, they may infect another individual. This is one of the reasons, of course, why drinking water must be purified with such care and why cholera and other forms of food poisoning are so much more common in slum areas where insanitary conditions prevail—or for that matter in times of war when normal standards of hygiene may have to be lowered.

Finally, there are the diseases such as the common cold and flu that are transmitted through the air directly from one person to the lungs of the next. Some of these diseases can spread through a population like wild fire. Epidemiologists have spent years in trying to unravel the processes by which these epidemics are propagated and some statisticians have drawn the parallel between the way in which such epidemics spread and the way in which rumors spread. The same, all important factor is involved in both cases: one person must spread the disease or rumor to at least one other person who has not previously heard the rumor or contracted the disease. If this happens, the epidemic will continue to grow; if it does not happen, the epidemic will begin to die out.

All the diseases I have mentioned in this chapter are of relevance to biological warfare, as are a number of other but much rarer diseases which we will meet in due course. We have seen that many of them have had a direct bearing on social evolution and on the history of man. It is not altogether surprising therefore that these diseases should also be seen as a potential military weapon. Any disease which can prevent a canal from being built, which can put half the labor force of a country out of action or which can cause massive emigration is clearly producing effects comparable even to the use of nuclear weapons. We should remember, too, that naturally occurring disease puts more people out of action in a war than do the weapons with which the war is being fought; three out of every four American soldiers in hospital in Vietnam in 1967 were suffering not from injuries but from naturally occurring illness. Clearly, disease can be a potent military force.

People have often assumed that biological weapons would be easy to use. This is not necessarily true for, as we have also seen, diseases spread in a multitude of ways and are caused by a great variety of microorganisms with widely varying characteristics. Each disease, therefore, represents a potential weapon in its own right and each will require specialized techniques if it is to be exploited in war. But, perhaps fortunately, diseases have been viewed as man's major enemy for much longer than politicians have sought to devise ways of using them in warfare. And although our current rate of spending on research into biological weapons may be large, the total so far spent is minute compared to the sums that have been lavished on improving our defense against disease. For the moment, then, we know a good deal more about the medical aspects of disease than we do about the military ones. Largely as a result of this, human populations are not now threatened with disease on anything like the scale which they were 50 or 100 years ago. It may have been easy to spread smallpox among the American Indians in the 18th century but it would be incomparably more difficult to repeat the process in the present-day United States. But it may be that this is only a temporary situation. As we shall see in the next chapter, the technical difficulties of using biological weapons are being studied extremely carefully. There is no cause for complacency and no reason to doubt that biological weapons will one day be perfected.

CHAPTER 5

Public Health in Reverse

A single ounce of the toxic agent which causes the disease called "Q-fever" would be sufficient to infect 28 billion people.

Brig. Gen. J. H. Rothschild
Harper's magazine (June 1959)

IT HAS BEEN ESTIMATED that it would take a million million million polio viruses to fill a Ping-Pong ball. Behind this staggering statement lies the basic reason that makes biological warfare such a grave potential threat. That Ping-Pong ball contains a great deal of infective material. Indeed, were it packed with some other more infectious but slightly larger virus, it would contain sufficient to infect, in theory, several thousand million million people (the present population of the world is a little over 3,000 million).

But although the potential threat is very great indeed, the practical possibilities of developing agents that could be used in military combat are limited by many complex and interacting factors. For example, an organism must be selected that can be grown in sufficient quantity and purity in the laboratory. The organisms should also be highly infectious and virulent—that is, a very small number of them should be capable of infecting man with a serious disease. The organism should be highly stable so that if it is dispersed in an aerosol spray from an aircraft, bomb, or rocket it will remain active for a period of several hours at least—by which time there is a reasonable chance that it will have found an opportunity to establish itself in a human host. It must also be stable when stored between production and delivery.

There are even more limitations affecting the disease itself. It must produce its effects quickly—within a few days at most—and must therefore be an acute one. The effects themselves must be severe, either killing the victim or incapacitating him for at least several days. The enemy should not be able to treat the disease easily with antibiotics or any other drugs. Nor must he have an appreciable natural immunity to the disease or be able to protect the population by vaccination. On the other hand, it would be extremely helpful if the attacking force could treat the disease and if they could also vaccinate themselves against it. Clearly, some of the requirements of an efficient, biological agent are to some extent self-contradictory; those very properties that make the agent suitable in one respect may well make it unsuitable in another.

The basic attraction of biological warfare to military thinkers is that far less material is needed to harm the enemy than is required when using other toxic but nonliving materials such as the nerve gases. The reason for this is not so much that a single virus or bacterium is itself very damaging but that once it becomes established inside a host it may reproduce with astonishing rapidity. In biological warfare, then, one is trying to exploit the capacity of all living organisms for self-replication. Inevitably, there is an exception to this generalization and, as I have not mentioned it before, it will be as well to deal with it at this stage.

Many bacteria exert their harmful effects on the human body by manufacturing and releasing complex chemical substances known as toxins. And some of these, as their name suggests, are incredibly toxic. We need concern ourselves here with only one—the botulinum toxin, which is produced by the bacterium *Clostridium botulinum*. This bacterium can live and grow only in the absence of oxygen. It is therefore found in nature only in soil, in mud at the bottom of the sea, and occasionally in the intestines of fish, including salmon. Like the anthrax bacterium, however, it can exist in the form of extremely hardy spores capable of withstanding up to six hours in boiling water. In spite of modern food processing techniques the bacterium does therefore very occasionally find its way into food—usually as a result of faulty preserving techniques used in the home. The bacterium first survives a spell in a normal atmosphere as a spore and then reverts to its vegetative form when it gets incorporated into the oxygen-free atmosphere of, say, a preserving jar. Although the absence of oxygen prevents most bacteria from multiplying, these are the conditions to which *C. botulinum* is best adapted. It therefore grows and begins to secrete the toxins into the food. If the food is not heated before serving, the toxins will be ingested; if it is heated, the toxins will be destroyed.

The toxins themselves are proteins of which six different types have so far been discovered—A, B, C, D, E, and F. The first two are the most toxic, and the lethal dose to humans of Type A is currently assessed at about 0.12 micrograms (12 hundred-millionths of a gram). This toxin, then, is one of the most noxious substances known. One ounce of it would be sufficient to kill 60 million people. On this basis, an ounce or two of the toxin introduced into a reservoir of 10 million gallons would, in theory, be sufficient to kill anyone who drank half a pint of water from the reservoir. This certainly implies that a few pounds of the material would be sufficient to contaminate the water supply of a large city. Any such contamination, however, would not be likely to get past water purification authorities unnoticed unless standards of public hygiene had first been reduced to a low level—for instance, by bombing the relevant buildings. In that case, or if the contamination were detected, the public would be instructed to boil all water before use; as the toxin is relatively sensitive to heat, this would remove most of the danger.

The fact that only a few dozen cases of botulism occur in the world every year gives some idea of how rarely the toxin gains access to human food. But when it does the effects are severe and rapid. There is a 60-70 percent mortality and the victims ultimately die from respiratory paralysis. The toxin acts by interfering with the action of nerves and muscles. When this effect reaches the diaphragm, which controls respiration, the victim dies from lack of oxygen. It is, of course, only the toxin that produces this effect and unless the bacterium is first given a chance to live in an oxygen free atmosphere it will not produce any toxin. Furthermore, it is extremely easy to denature and thus inactivate the toxin. This requires only gentle heating for a few minutes. Botulism poisoning occurs only after foods such as cold meat, fish, or canned vegetables are eaten without further cooking immediately before serving. There is no effective treatment for the poisoning, although antitoxins do exist which may help if given very soon after the toxin is ingested. If given in advance, antitoxins also give protection against the toxin, but they are used only by laboratory workers who are studying the toxins or the bacteria which produce them.

The toxin was first isolated in pure form during World War II by scientists at the United States center for research into biological warfare known then as Camp Detrick and now as Fort Detrick. The toxin clearly is a potential weapon though whether it is more strictly classified as a chemical or a biological one is difficult to decide (it is the toxin, not the bacteria, which would be distributed). It can be stored in airtight containers for indefinite periods. It produces severe and rapid action yet is decomposed on exposure to air within about 12 hours, so that invading troops could then move in with complete safety. It cannot be treated and there is no natural immunity against it. According to one report, certain Canadian troops during the last war were told that if they were captured they were to give the enemy their name, number, and the information that they had been inoculated with botulinum toxoid. This was a piece of psychological gamesmanship designed to make the enemy believe that the Allies' knowledge of the toxin was advanced and that the material was sufficiently developed to be used as a weapon. Serious consideration was also given as to whether the Germans might oppose D-Day landings with attacks with the toxin. The threat was particularly real because the toxin can be disseminated in an aerosol spray and it is about 1,000 times more toxic when inhaled as when ingested.

The botulinum toxin is certainly one of the most toxic chemicals known. Compared with living organisms, however, relatively large amounts of it are required to produce death. Type A toxin, as I have said, has a molecular weight of one million or so and a huge number of these molecular weights is needed to cause death in man. Some diseases, on the other hand, can be caused by the inhalation of a single virus particle and some viruses have molecular weights of less than one million. Some forms of living matter are therefore clearly much more "toxic."

Scientists use two terms to assess the toxicity of living material. One is infectivity, which is the dose of material required to set up a spreading infection in the host—for the organism to establish itself there and begin to reproduce. Virulence, the other term, is a measure of the damaging effects produced when a small dose of organisms initiates infection—in other words, this term also reflects the nature of the disease that is produced. It is important to distinguish between these terms for we are constantly being infected by highly infectious bacteria and viruses which display little or no virulence; these are harmless organisms that would have no biological warfare applications. Only if an organism has both high infectivity and virulence can it be considered as a possible military agent.

Unless a disease is easily curable—in which case there may be limitations to its use as a biological agent—it is very difficult to establish the infectivity of the organism which causes it in man. Occasionally, when accidental infection occurs in the laboratory, it is possible to assess roughly what dose the victim received and thus make a guess at its infectivity. But this is not an accurate method and scientists will accept such figures only if they are averages obtained from a number of experiments. Inevitably, then, most of our information about infectivity is obtained from work on animals such as rats, mice, and guinea pigs. Such experiments have shown that some diseases may be produced when only a single organism— a single bacterium or virus—is inhaled. Smallpox (more accurately, a certain strain of it) is one of these and dengue fever—a viral disease that produces intense aching over many parts of the body—another. Among the bacterial diseases, tularemia (infective aerosol dose 25 organisms) and brucellosis are produced by extremely infective organisms. So, too, is Q-fever which is produced by an organism known as a rickettsia which shares some of the properties of both viruses and bacteria and is classified by microbiologists as a separate class of microorganism, falling somewhere between viruses and bacteria. A single Q-fever organism is thought to be sufficient to initiate infection. Plague and glanders can both be caused by a dose of about 3,000 organisms. The infectivity of diseases which are spread by insect bites can also be high but in natural conditions only one piece of information is strictly relevant; a single mosquito bite is sufficient to cause infection with, say, yellow fever. Clearly, with a highly infective organism it is theoretically possible to infect a sizable population with very little material indeed.

Infectivity is not a property of microorganisms that can never be changed. On the contrary, it is a highly variable characteristic and the examples of high infectivity which I have given apply only to "ideal" conditions and to selected strains of the organisms. They refer to healthy individuals; sick people may be more easily infected or may show an unexpectedly high resistance. They also refer to doses that are administered through the respiratory route of infection. Inhalation, and injection through the skin, are often much more effective ways of spreading disease than ingestion; organisms sometimes have quite low infectivity if they are ingested with food or drink, even though they may be highly infective if inhaled.

I have dealt with infectivity at some length because it is crucial to the arguments of why one should want to use biological agents in war at all—that a minute amount of biological material can kill or incapacitate large numbers of people. Virulence is equally important as a direct measure of the clinical results that the disease will produce when it is actually used. Perhaps the third most important property is stability. A highly virulent and infective organism will clearly be of no use if it is killed rapidly upon exposure to the atmosphere or upon dissemination from a missile or bomb. The other required properties of biological agents—such as resistance to antibiotics—are of secondary importance. Like the primary properties, they depend a great deal on the way in which the biological weapon is manufactured, stored, and disseminated but they are a good deal easier to change. For instance, there are now many naturally occurring strains of organisms that are resistant to treatment with the antibiotic normally used for that purpose. A strain of the tularemia organism resistant to streptomycin is available in the laboratory, as is a strain of anthrax resistant to certain antibiotics; similar strains of other organisms can be grown in cultures containing very weak solutions of the antibiotic, which selects mutants able to grow in the presence of the drug.

There is no fundamental problem about growing bacteria, viruses, and other organisms in the laboratory. Viruses and rickettsiae, of course, can reproduce only within the living cells of a host and so can be grown only in cultures of isolated cells such as fertilized chicken eggs. Bacteria can be grown much more simply in a "nutrient broth" or some other suitable medium which can provide the necessary raw materials which the bacteria need to survive. Techniques for growing microorganisms have now reached a high degree of sophistication. One of the most important advances in this field was made by scientists at the M.R.E. in Porton who succeeded in producing continuous cultures of cells. Previously cells could be grown only in batches. When placed in a nutrient medium, they

would soon begin to reproduce and establish a fast growing colony of cells. But eventually, as the supply of nutrient dropped and side products built up, the rate of
growth slowed down and finally stopped. The cells which
were produced in this way were of varying ages, differed
in other characteristics and were of limited total yield. But
with very accurate control of the conditions used, and by
passing nutrients continually through the container and
drawing off side products, the Porton scientists succeeded in establishing a means for growing cells that was
continuous and which yielded cells at a constant rate and
with constant characteristics. The technique has since
been taken up by laboratories all over the world and is
now widely used in the pharmaceutical industry.

Viruses and rickettsiae can often be grown best in cells
derived not from a fully grown animal but from their em-
bryos. This is one of the reasons why fertilized chicken
eggs are used extensively on an industrial basis for the
production of virus vaccines against such diseases as yellow fever and flu. In fact many of our antiviral vaccines
come from virus that has been grown in chicken eggs—
and in one case duck eggs, which take longer to hatch.
The others are grown in tissue cultures, sometimes of human embryonic cells. There are still some microorganisms
that cannot be grown in the laboratory—such as the organism that causes syphilis and the virus that produces
hepatitis—but nearly all the diseases that are of relevance
to biological warfare are caused by organisms which can
be grown in this way.

The problem, however, is to grow them in a form which
retains the desired properties of the organisms, or if the
properties are unsuitable to start with, which changes
their properties in the right way. Nearly all microorganisms are very susceptible to change when grown in arti-

ficial media. Sometimes this can be exploited by scientists interested in developing a biological weapon. The potency of botulinum toxin Type E, for instance, is increased 40-400 times if the parent bacteria are grown in a medium containing the pancreatic enzyme trypsin at pH 6-7 (slightly acidic conditions). But more often the virulence of the strain will be decreased when it is grown in an artificial medium, as happens if the viruses of yellow fever or smallpox are grown in tissue culture at room temperature or slightly higher. A virulent strain of smallpox, for instance, is available but its virulence can be maintained only if it is grown in a culture of human embryo tissue; grown in any other tissue culture it will lose its virulence. The environment in which a microorganism is grown may also affect other properties. For instance, changing the source of the yeast extract used to provide a medium for the growth of one of the bacteria that produces brucellosis has been found to produce organisms that survive better in a damp atmosphere than in a dry one. The microorganism which produces plague is also environment sensitive. It survives much longer when dispersed in an aerosol cloud if the medium in which it was grown contained only a low concentration of chloride ions. On the other hand, if chloride ions are rigorously excluded from the nutrient the bacteria grow more slowly.

It is here that the military microbiologist must use the most subtle of the scientific skills which he has mastered. Virtually none of the naturally occurring, disease-causing organisms possesses the complete spectrum of properties which would make it a "perfect" biological agent; in almost every case there is some property—stability or virulence, for instance—which must be altered if the organism is to be used as a biological weapon. Can such organisms be invested with these new properties?

The answer is yes and no—yes, they can certainly be given new properties but, no, it is not always easy to invest them with the right new ones. Let us consider virulence first. The basis of much of today's vaccine production is the breeding of weakened or attenuated strains of viruses. These strains differ from one another genetically but the chemical difference may be marginal: the difference between a mild strain and a virulent one may be no more than the replacement of just three of the five million or so atoms which make up a particular virus. These molecular changes are brought about by chance mutations, possibly as a result of radiation which is always present on the earth. In theory all that is required to find a virulent strain is to keep the organism growing and to divide it into batches from time to time. Each time the new batches are tested for virulence and eventually it will be found that a mutation has occurred in one and that this strain is now more virulent than the others.

In practice the process is much more complicated and far more time consuming. The organism is often passaged through series after series of animals or tissue cultures until the required strain is found. An example from preventive medicine—as distinct from military medicine— shows just how complex the process can become.

In 1934 Dr. Max Theiler, as I have already mentioned, set himself the unenviable task of trying to find a better vaccine against yellow fever than the one that was in use. Theiler first performed 17 series of tissue culture experiments, growing the yellow fever virus in each. In the 17th he used a particularly virulent strain of yellow fever known as the Asibi virus. Theiler kept this virus alive for three years without ever passing it through an animal host, which was no mean achievement in 1934. The strain was grown in a variety of different tissues. One line was origi-

nally grown in mouse embryo tissues but was later transferred to whole chicken embryo tissue, which had been
minced up. It was passed through the chicken culture 58
times and then divided up into three batches. One was
continued as before, one was grown in chick embryo
brain alone, and the third was grown in chick embryo
that had had the brain and spinal cord removed. This
third culture was then continued through another 118 sub-
cultures. It was then tested again on monkeys—from
which it was originally derived—and it was found that,
unlike the original strains, it did not kill them. Indeed, one
month later the monkeys were found to be immune to the
original wild virus strain. It was this strain that later became the standard one for yellow fever vaccine for every-
where except Africa.

The way in which this strain was produced is not quite
so haphazard as it might appear. An organism tends to
adapt itself, through natural selection, to the environment in which it lives. Thus if a strain is particularly virulent when injected into brain, you grow it in tissue that
does not contain brain if you want to develop an attenuated virus. If you want a virulent virus, on the other
hand, you play your cards in the reverse order—you grow
it in the kind of tissue which you particularly want it to
attack: human embryo tissue in the case of biological warfare agents. In a similar way, if you want an agent that is
resistant to a certain antibiotic you grow a strain of that
agent in a culture that contains a very dilute solution of
the antibiotic.

Such a technique is obviously time consuming. Methods
are available for increasing the rate of mutation—notably
the application of radiation and certain chemical agents
—but these techniques normally produce strains of lowered rather than increased virulence. And there is no

known method which will give rise to mutations producing a desired effect. Mutations occur randomly and the best that can be done is to arrange the conditions of the experiment so that the required strains have a better chance of surviving than do the strains that are not required. The difficulty here is that it is often not possible to select for more than two or three of the properties that are required at the same time. There are at least a dozen important requirements of any biological agent, and in breeding one which fulfills the stability requirement, for instance, one may also be producing a strain that is of low infectivity. One has to select for all the required properties at the same time.

There are, however, other even more sophisticated means of changing the properties of biological agents. Although bacteria normally reproduce quite simply by splitting in two, they can be made to combine sexually. During this conjugation process the two bacteria are connected to one another by a thin bridge of tissue and part of the genetic material of the male bacterium is passed to the female. As even bacteria of different strains can conjugate sexually, this method offers the theoretical possibility of passing properties such as high virulence from one strain of bacterium to another. Although I have been assured by microbiologists that so far this technique has not produced strains of increased virulence—the reverse seems to be the general rule—the technique may eventually find applications in biological warfare. It has already been established that resistance to antibiotics can be transferred from one strain of bacterium to another in this way. Bacterial conjugation is one of a number of subtle techniques at the frontiers of our current knowledge, which may or may not produce alarming results in the future. Another is the ability of certain viruses living in bacteria to transfer genetic material from one bacterial cell to another. Here again there are no known military applications—yet.

The ultimate in sophisticated military microbiology, of course, would be the creation of an entirely artificial form of life that produced some quite unknown disease. There is a popular misconception about biological warfare that the principal aim is to do just this. This is not true; indeed, the creation of life in the test tube is still far out of reach of our most advanced microbiological techniques. Experts currently assess that such a breakthrough is not likely before the late 1980s or early 1990s. There are, therefore, far more immediate worries connected with biological warfare and the fact that the creation of test-tube organisms is still distant does not reduce the severity of the problem by very much. It is as well to remember that although biological agents must be chosen from the organisms that cause the 160 or so known infectious diseases, each of these organisms can exist in many different strains. In 1959, for instance, more than 140 different strains of *Pasteurella pestis*—the bacterium that causes plague—had been identified. A wide choice of material is therefore already known and more advanced microbiological techniques are likely to make it wider still.

From what has been said it should be clear that the development of strains of microorganisms of potential use in biological warfare is a complex business. It requires the use of techniques that lie at the forefront of modern science and medicine and the skills of highly trained scientists and doctors capable of using these techniques. But these people are not using the techniques in a conventional way. They are, in fact, using them to achieve the exact opposite of the purpose for which they were originally devised. The applications of modern microbiology are normally thought to lie in the domain of public health. Scientists working at biological warfare research centers are striving to achieve exactly the opposite effect, by making microorganisms more stable, more virulent, and more infective. Their work has been aptly described as "public health in reverse."

I hope I have now indicated something of the difficulties surrounding the development of a strain of virus or bacterium capable of being used effectively in biological warfare. But suppose such a strain has been developed, or is in the near future. How easy would it be to produce enough living material to use as a weapon? Unhappily, there is no real problem about producing microorganisms in quantity. For one thing, the quantities needed are relatively small compared with any other weapon, even nuclear devices. A fraction of a gram of purified bacteria or virus dispersed in aerosol form could be sufficient to infect anyone in a square kilometer who breathed the aerosol unprotected for a few minutes.

At the most, this would require only a few kilograms of "starting material"—that is, the unpurified products that are obtained in a tissue culture or by growing bacteria in a nutrient medium. In theory one gram of chicken embryo tissue, inoculated with the Q-fever organism, would be sufficient to infect more than one million people. But we must remember that a large proportion of the organisms contained in that gram of material will be inactivated by the time it has been purified, stored, transported, loaded into an actual weapon, dispersed, and come in contact with its target. A large-scale biological attack would require kilogram quantities of the unpurified starting material. How long would it take to produce this amount of material?

There are, of course, no figures available for the time required to produce biological weapons as such. But we do know a lot about the generation times—the time required for a bacterial population to double its size—of individual bacteria. One kilogram (dry weight) of the harmless bacterium *Escherichia coli* can be produced in the laboratory in 24 hours. Suspensions of *Brucella melitensis* (one of the organisms which produces brucellosis) have been made which contain 10,000 million organisms per milliliter at a rate of half a liter every few hours. Although the actual rate of production, which is governed by the generation times of the organisms, could not be increased by scaling up these processes from laboratory size to semi-industrial output, the total output could certainly be increased. Indeed manufacture of virus material is already carried out on an industrial scale by pharmaceutical firms. Polio vaccine, for instance, has been produced in 1,200 liter batches. Ironically enough, the preparation of large, purified batches of vaccine has recently been speeded up by equipment originally developed in the atomic weapons program. Known as the zonal ultra-centrifuge, this equipment is a means of centrifuging large volumes of material at very high speed; it was developed in the hope that it could be used to separate uranium isotopes required for nuclear weapons. The centrifuge is now being adopted by industry and it is enabling firms to produce larger batches of purified vaccine more quickly than was previously possible.

Once the right strain of organism had been selected, and the optimum conditions found for growing it, sufficiently large quantities of it to infect huge areas could certainly be produced within a week and quite probably within three or four days. This being the case, there does not appear to be any great need to store the material for long periods. Such material can be stored, with difficulty, by refrigeration or by freeze drying techniques for several weeks. Additives can also be used to help stabilize the product; the brucellosis bacteria, for instance, are stabilized if kept in a medium containing dextrin and protein decomposition products. If the agents are kept for a long time, of course, their infectivity or virulence will certainly decrease; indeed if no protective measures are taken 80-90 percent of the organisms will probably die within a matter of hours. But a strain with high storage stability could certainly be produced and delivered within a matter of days. The circumstances that might lead to biological warfare are not likely to be similar to those that could lead to nuclear war, requiring retaliation within a matter of minutes; "off-the-peg" biological agents are not likely to be required and they would be produced as and when needed.

The "ideal" biological agent would have three properties which I have not yet mentioned in detail but which must be given serious consideration before the agent is selected and manufactured. They are these: there should be no natural immunity against the disease being used; the enemy should not possess or be able to produce a vaccine against it; and he should not be able to cure it with, say, antibiotics. On the other hand, it would clearly be a great advantage if the attacking force had the necessary antibiotic and it is normally regarded as essential that he has large stocks of an appropriate vaccine to protect his troops, and possibly his civilians in case the agent should become retroactive and spread back into friendly territory.

The relationship of natural immunity to biological warfare is a complex one, as are so many of the factors involved in this form of war. One thing, at any rate, is clear: it would be useless to disseminate any disease against which there is widespread natural immunity. The virulent forms of measles and mumps, for instance, can produce severely incapacitating diseases but the majority of populations have suffered from them already and are unlikely to succumb to a second infection. Poliomyelitis, too, has probably been contracted by most people in a mild form without their ever realizing it; as a result they are now immune to the disease. Three natural forms of the polio virus are known and in the United States immunity to one or more of them extends to between 15 and 85 percent of the population, depending on the area concerned. But even of those who contract the disease, only 0.1 to 5 percent later become paralyzed. For these and other reasons polio is not a disease that is considered among the likely contenders for biological warfare. On the other hand, diseases which are naturally extremely rare, such as tularemia or melioidosis, are likely to be much more effective as biological agents.

By far the most vigorous defense against both chemical and biological attack would be to use protective drugs or vaccinations in advance of any possible attack. Currently there seems little chance of being able to protect troops or civilians against the whole range of material which might be used. If intelligence networks could reveal the most likely agents, however, there is more hope of massive vaccination programs against, say, two or three diseases.

There are several ways of protecting against disease. The two most generally effective are the administration of live and attenuated vaccines. Such vaccines, as I have mentioned, have been prepared against a number of diseases but by no means all. By and large, it is much easier to prepare vaccines against the viral diseases than it is against the bacterial ones. Vaccines against three possible virus diseases—polio, smallpox, and yellow fever— are already in mass production. There are few important virus diseases for which some form of vaccination is not available—although it is not always available in large quantities or effective for long periods. The only vaccine in widespread use against a bacterial disease of possible military significance is that for cholera—which is rather an unusual type of bacterium in any case; but the effects of the vaccine are short-lived and it must be renewed every six months. Vaccines have been produced against brucellosis, anthrax, plague, and tularemia but they are not widely used and, by and large, are not very effective (an ineffective vaccine is one that produces protection for a limited period of time, against a relatively small proportion of those vaccinated or produces rather common and serious side effects—or, of course, all three). This certainly suggests that the bacterial diseases have at least one major advantage over viral diseases as military weapons.

There is an opportunity here for a form of psychological warfare which might be called biological blackmail. During the mid-1960s the World Health Organization estimated that the current costs of smallpox vaccination in Europe and in the United States were between $43 million and $70 million annually. The cost of immunizing a whole population against just one disease—to which the cost of developing the vaccine may also have to be added—will therefore be huge. Strategists must certainly have examined the consequences of this, for if an enemy could be frightened into vaccinating a population against, say, two or three diseases, the cost might certainly exert a noticeable effect on her total war effort. The psychological effect on the population might also be disturbing.

If from an immunological point of view the bacterial diseases offer better prospects of providing biological agents than do the viral diseases, the reverse applies when we consider therapy: generally, it is much easier to cure bacterial diseases than viral ones. This is due almost entirely to the development of antibiotics since World War II. These substances, sometimes synthetic, sometimes the natural products of fungi or other forms of life, are tailormade to attack certain classes of bacteria or other simple microorganisms. They do so by interfering grossly with the metabolic machinery of the bacterium. Some will attack a fairly wide range of bacteria and others are designed or have been modified to kill only a single species. They are of very limited effectiveness against the viruses, however.

The great therapeutic breakthrough against viral diseases is still awaited and for this reason most of the viral diseases can be treated only by what the medical profession terms "supportive treatment." In effect, this means tucking the patient up in bed, taking his temperature regularly and generally making him as comfortable as possible. Drugs such as cortisone can tide the patient over in the face of some viral diseases, but they are not as effective as are the antibiotics against the bacterial diseases. With some viral diseases, such as flu and the common cold, this yawning gap in modern therapy is not of great consequence. The patient almost always recovers in a few days providing that these complaints do not so weaken the body that other more serious infections begin to build up. (This, incidentally, was one of the gravest aftereffects of mustard poisoning during World War I; mustard so damaged the lungs that subsequent bacterial infections led to pneumonia or tuberculosis).

With other virus diseases, the result is much more severe. Nothing much can be done to cure a patient with polio, smallpox, or yellow fever, for instance. Antivirus therapy is, of course, the subject of huge research programs in the laboratories of pharmaceutical firms throughout the world but there are unhappily no real signs of a breakthrough on the scale of the antibacterial drugs.

This is not the place to consider in any further detail the current medical treatment for the complete range of infectious disease; much more detail is available from any medical text book. Such information, however, could turn out to be almost irrelevant in the event of biological warfare. If the disease can be cured, if the drug to cure it is stockpiled in huge quantities, and if it can cure it in as little as two days, a biological weapon might still produce its intended effect. If the objective were to take a city, or move through a jungle, the operation might be complete in just the time it took to cure the disease with even the most efficient drug. (The attacking force would, of course, have to delay until the incubation period was complete). Prevention is proverbially better than cure and in biological warfare it might be a great deal better: it might mean the difference between victory and defeat.

Having said something about the properties required of a biological agent in war, it is now possible to speculate in more detail about those diseases that might be used. There are two important sources of this information. The first is the purely scientific data which I have been discussing; the stringent requirements that must be made of a biological agent rule out many naturally occurring diseases and suggest a number of likely candidates for biological warfare. But this information exists only in a vacuum and might be untrustworthy could it not be supported by information about the range of diseases on which biological warfare centers are working. Fortunately, this other kind of information is also available because such centers publish most of their work that could be relevant to medical research. A survey of the papers published by scientists at biological warfare centers in the United States and the United Kingdom, for instance, shows that centers are indeed working on those very diseases which a purely scientific analysis of the problems involved suggests they would be. Thus the information which follows can be taken as largely reliable though inevitably there will be minor inconsistencies between it and the real situation.

But there is another problem. When we get down to naming names we can discuss only the properties of the agents as they exist in nature and not the details of the new strains which have undoubtedly been produced in biological warfare research centers. For this reason such a discussion can be misleading and I must emphasize that when talking about the individual diseases in the next section I shall refer mainly to naturally occurring strains; if only one or two properties of these strains have been altered in the laboratory, this might be sufficient to turn an otherwise unpromising organism into an effective biological weapon.

That said, however, we can start off on firm ground with botulinum toxin. If any biological weapon is stockpiled, or held in constant readiness by a nation, it is most likely to be botulinum toxin. And this in itself is a paradox which highlights the drawbacks of biological weapons; botulinum toxin could, possibly with more accuracy, be called a chemical agent rather than a biological one. The toxin itself is not living in any sense of the word and it is incapable of reproducing itself. But botulinum toxin is considered as a possible weapon simply on the strength of its high toxicity. By common agreement it is classed as a biological weapon and not a chemical one because it is derived from biological material. But, because it is not living, its dissemination presents few of the problems associated with true biological material. It can be handled much more harshly without affecting its potency and, of course, there is absolutely no danger of it spreading back to the force that originally used it. Indeed, in the atmosphere it decomposes in a convenient 12 hours leaving the area uncontaminated. The lethal dose is very low—much less than one millionth of a gram—and the mortality rate is high. Botulism is impossible to cure and, because it is not a disease, there is no natural resistance to it. On the other hand, a toxoid is available that will give protection. Botulinum toxin offers most of the characteristics required of a biological agent. It can be produced in quantity and can be stored indefinitely in airtight containers. It is the most controllable of the biological agents and, if biological weapons *are* ever used, it—or some other similar bacterial toxin—is quite likely to be the first to move from the development laboratory to the field of operations.

The doubts about reliability and effectiveness which I have already mentioned affect all the other potential biological weapons. Let us consider the virus diseases first. The laboratory cultivation of viruses is more difficult than that of bacteria but nevertheless can be accomplished either in human or monkey cells, or in fertilized chicken eggs. But the virus is not a metabolic organism—it does not need and indeed cannot utilize food. For that reason it is unable to repair any damage which may arise; viruses, as a class, are therefore more liable to irreversible damage than are bacteria, but there are exceptions. Furthermore, most of them produce longer lasting immunity in their hosts and hence give prolonged protection against a second attack. There is likely therefore to be more widespread natural immunity against viruses than against bacteria. These, then, are some of the drawbacks of using virus diseases as biological weapons. Against them must be set the fact that antibiotics, so effective against bacterial diseases, are almost useless against viral diseases.

The respiratory viruses are perhaps the most common. They cause the common cold, flu and some forms of pneumonia. But their effects are generally so mild—considered in terms of what the military regard as "incapacitating"—that they would be of little effect in warfare. They are so widely distributed that there must be considerable immunity against them, a conclusion which is supported by the common sense observation that, when flu or the common cold gets a grip in winter, even the harshest epidemics strike down considerably less than one fifth of the population at any time; indeed, an epidemic that did infect one person in five would be severe indeed. The fact that the respiratory viruses are among the most stable will therefore count for little unless a virulent strain has been developed which produces far more severe effects than those usually found. But, all in all, the respiratory viruses rank low in the biological warfare league table.

The viruses which infect the intestine, such as the polio viruses, are also relatively stable. They can cause severe effects and death in a large proportion of those unfortunate enough to succumb to the diseases which they produce. But a limitation on these viruses as biological weapons is that most of us acquire immunity to them very early in life. This provides lasting resistance to much more virulent forms of the same disease. These viruses seem only a little bit more likely to be of military use than the respiratory ones.

A whole range of viruses is transmitted by animal vectors. These include yellow fever, dengue or breakbone fever, several different forms of encephalitis, and many others. If these viruses were to be used in biological war, they might have to be "separated" from their animal hosts and delivered in aerosol form. But most of them at least are extremely unstable when exposed to the air. Over the millennia, as might be expected, they have become adapted to their animal or human hosts and have not evolved any specific adaptations to survive outside these protective environments. So although the vector viruses are easily cultured, they have other, more profound, drawbacks as military agents unless they are to be spread together with their animal vectors.

I have left the smallpox virus to last because it is one of the more likely of the viruses to make a biological agent. Although there are doubts about its stability, it is lethal, extremely virulent, and highly infective. It can cause infection via the respiratory route and it is confined to a relatively small portion of the world. It is extremely rare in Europe and the United States; this is often assumed to be a result of the massive smallpox vaccination campaigns that have been undertaken in these two areas. But this is not strictly true for figures now available show that only about one half of these populations has ever been vaccinated against smallpox. Furthermore, many of those who have been vaccinated are not necessarily now immune to the disease as the effects of the vaccination may have worn off. In fact only about one third of the population of Europe and the United States is now believed to be immune to smallpox. The disease is rare in these areas because very strict legislation exists forbidding entry of anyone who has come from a smallpox area unless he has been vaccinated a specified number of days before arrival. In this way the entry of the smallpox virus itself is strictly controlled and the need for vaccination has become less real. As a result an aggressor might find smallpox one of the more efficient diseases to use in an attack against either Europe or the United States. The same arguments would apply to any other disease which would normally be prevalent in an area, which is prevented from establishing itself by immigration laws, and against which a large proportion of the population has not been vaccinated. Indeed, this artificial means of preventing the immigration of viruses or bacteria may even mean that a population is less immune to the disease than it would normally be; there is likely to be low resistance to any disease that has been unknown in an area for some decades.

Until recently, scientists assumed that the organism that causes psittacosis, or parrot fever, was also a virus. A glance at the properties of the agent (Table II) shows that if it were a virus it would be a most unusual one. For one thing, psittacosis is much more responsive to antibiotic treatment than are most other viral diseases. For another, it has not proved possible to develop a really effective vaccine against the disease. Scientists have now classed the organism in a different group from both viruses and bacteria. It is a group containing the trachoma organism, the agent that produces such a devastating eye disease over large portions of the underdeveloped world.

The symptoms of parrot fever are a mild to severe pneumonia, which is sometimes lethal. It is not naturally a particularly common disease, which is surprising for there is good evidence that it is carried by many species of birds, including both pigeons and parrots (hence the name parrot fever). It can be extremely infective and immunity to it is rare. In many ways, psittacosis might make an ideal biological agent, although there are several points about which there is still room for doubt. One is its stability, which is not known with any accuracy; another is that the disease can be treated with antibiotics, which might weigh against it. It is clear, however, that it is widely considered by personnel at biological warfare research centers to be a potential biological weapon; its name crops up frequently in the scientific literature which these centers publish and it is often talked about when biological warfare experts give their views in public.

Another class of agent being studied for biological warfare is the rickettsia—organisms intermediate in structure between bacteria and viruses but which, like the latter, can reproduce only within the cell of a host. The two most widely known members of the group are those that produce typhus and Q-fever. Both suffer from the principal disadvantage of the viruses: because they are well adapted to life inside their hosts—which can be man or other animals, particularly ticks—they are not very stable when exposed on their own to the environment. The Q-fever organism is assumed to be slightly better in this respect than the typhus organism but whether it is sufficiently stable to survive lengthy dissemination in an aerosol spray is another matter. Both organisms, however, are extremely infective and produce severe effects which are often fatal (more often for typhus than for Q-fever). Both can be treated with antibiotics and effective vaccines are available in large quantities against both diseases. The Q-fever organism is reputed to be more stable in storage than the organism that produces epidemic typhus. But really the same factors that make vector borne viruses such a poor bet as biological agents apply to both typhus and to Q-fever. Both organisms are well adapted to insect hosts—ticks and lice—and unless they can be substantially altered to survive in a way quite alien to their natural existence they might be relatively useless in a biological aerosol.

Jumping up the biological scale of complexity, we should consider briefly those organisms larger than bacteria that also produce infectious disease. One group in particular is of relevance because, like the anthrax bacterium, they can form spores which will withstand a great deal of hardship. These are the fungi, belonging to the same group of organisms as the mushrooms and toad-stools and the much smaller variety that produces the ir-ritating disease known as athlete's foot. One fungal disease is particularly important: coccidioidomycosis, a usually mild but sometimes severe fever that produces fatalities only rarely. The disease itself is generally rare, even though the organism is highly infectious. This again sug-gests that there may be relatively high natural immunity against it. It is normally produced as a result of the spores of vegetative forms being inhaled; it is difficult to treat and there is no really satisfactory vaccine in use against it. Its one main advantage is the fact that, as a spore-forming organism, it could be disseminated as an aerosol without danger of greatly affecting its viability.

But by far the most important group of organisms to be considered as possible biological agents are the bac-teria. Of those that affect man alone, plague, tularemia, cholera, and melioidosis are perhaps the most likely agents. Except for cholera, all are extremely infective via the respiratory route. Melioidosis scores an extra point in that it is apparently resistant to most antibiotics, even in its naturally occurring strain (though prolonged treat-ment with Chloromycetin has been claimed effective). Al-though vaccines against these diseases do exist they are not (except for the short-term cholera vaccine) in mass production—and this, from the point of view of biological warfare, is perhaps the ideal situation, for it allows the attacker to give himself protection but probably does not afford the attacked sufficient time to develop and use a vaccine on a large scale. The devastating effects which plague can make on civilization have, as we have seen, been amply documented throughout history and particularly in the 14th century. All these diseases produce severe effects; they are sometimes or often fatal and melioidosis leads to mania and delirium. They are among the most unpleasant of the diseases likely to be used in biological warfare and, regrettably, among the most suitable.

Anthrax, brucellosis (or undulant fever), and glanders are also bacterial diseases and they have one other factor in common; they share both man and cattle as victims. They are unpleasant diseases, producing severe effects and often leading to death in their acute form. Anthrax is capable of forming extremely hardy spores which, as I have mentioned, have been used to contaminate Gruinard Island in Scotland for more than twenty years. Glanders and brucellosis are both highly infective and all three diseases are infective via the respiratory route. In most of the Western world they have been fairly rigorously controlled mainly because the source of the disease—cattle—comes into frequent contact with humans. In addition, of course, they represent a potential threat to livestock which, while perhaps not of the same importance as foot and mouth, is very real. Whether or not it would be sufficiently real to warrant the use of biological agents to infect both man and the animals on which he depends we shall see in Chapter 7.

CHAPTER 6

Spreading the Disease

Biological "fall-out," like radiation from a nuclear bomb, is capable of returning to bite the hand that launched it.

Louis E. Carlat
(*Nuclear Information*, Vol. 14, No. 4, February 1963.)

THE SINGLE most expensive items on the defense budgets of the advanced nations are the delivery systems for their weapons. They include fleets of Polaris submarines, supersonic stratospheric aircraft, and scores of different kinds of missiles. Clearly any new weapon system offering any hope of cutting down the costs incurred by the maintenance of these delivery systems will be viewed by defense authorities in a favorable light. As recently as 1959 Rothschild was complaining that the entire amount of money allotted to the U.S. Chemical Corps for research and development was less than the cost of two B-58 bombers. To some it seemed that the development of biological weapons might make all these delivery systems redundant. But a closer look at the available methods of delivering biological weapons shows that this is not the case. While acts of sabotage might be carried out by the "man on a bicycle," biological warfare proper would need the use of delivery systems just as sophisticated as those required

116

for nuclear weapons if the defenses of a country such as the United States or the Soviet Union were ever to be penetrated.

There are basically three ways in which a microorganism can infect its human host. The first means of penetration is through the skin, as occurs when a mosquito injects yellow fever virus or a doctor injects a yellow fever vaccine. The second is ingestion of the microorganisms with food or drink which, as we have seen, is the way in which botulism and cholera normally strike. The third is through the inhalation of the organisms as in the spread of pneumonic plague, flu, or smallpox.

There is obviously no chance of spreading a disease deliberately by infecting cuts or injecting large numbers of enemy troops. Consideration has been given, however, to establishing the diseases which are naturally carried by animals by releasing the infected animal vectors in large numbers and leaving them to transfer the disease to a human population. The Japanese devoted considerable research to this aspect of biological warfare in the 1930s and early 1940s. Details of some of this work were published in Japan in 1952, and pictures were shown of biological bombs consisting of canisters that would be dropped by parachute. When they hit the ground they would either break open, or open automatically, and release, say, plague-infected rats. The first requirement of this technique is a production facility for rearing huge numbers of infected animal vectors. Work on the problems involved is known to be going on in the United States centers for biological warfare research and one of the "opportunities" offered to scientists willing to work at Fort Detrick is the chance to carry out "basic studies of effects of rearing procedures for various insects on longevity and fecundity; the effects of different environmental factors on infection of insects and on virulence of microorganisms." Among the insects that have been held constantly available at Detrick are mosquitoes infected with yellow fever, malaria, and dengue; fleas infected with plague, ticks infected with tularemia, relapsing fever, and Colorado fever; and flies infected with cholera, anthrax, and dysentery.

During World War II the Japanese center in Manchuria was said to be capable of producing 45 liters of plague-infected fleas every four months. During this period some 135 million insects would have been produced and plans were even made for producing four times this quantity. Experiments with volunteers have suggested that malaria and dengue fever can be spread by the release of infected vectors and one experiment in a relatively mosquito-free area of Florida has shown that the release of 200,000 mosquitoes from special canisters produced many bites on a high percentage of people living in and near an adjacent air base within a few days. If the mosquitoes had been infected with Q-fever most of the local inhabitants would have contracted the disease.

But few experts on biological warfare now believe that this would be the most efficient means of disseminating disease. It would certainly be one of the most risky for it involves the inclusion of a third factor—the animal vector—into what is already a complex operation. There are many reasons why the dropping of these infected animals might produce no effect at all, the animals finding it impossible to establish themselves in their alien surroundings. If they did establish themselves, there is no reliable way of telling to what extent the disease would be transmitted to a human population. Their effect might be either negligible or, for that matter, it might get completely out of hand and go on to produce a pandemic of disease of the kind I described in Chapter 4. Although this is possible, it is unlikely because most modern armies (and civilian populations) are quite capable of exterminating vectors within their camps. In some parts of the world public hygiene is so good that the vectors would stand little chance of surviving. Furthermore, many of the relevant vectors are restricted to only tropical or subtropical areas of the world and this puts an immediate limitation on the effectiveness of the weapon. One is left, then, with a means of attack limited mainly to near equatorial regions with little or no public hygiene, an unknown chance of success in any event, and an attack that might infect only a small proportion of the population even if "successful."

The second method of dissemination might be to contaminate food or drink with infective material. This again is a technique that would be difficult to employ on a large scale. The only possibility of producing wide-scale disease in this way seems to be the contamination of food in a food processing plant or of water supplies in a reservoir. Even this would be very difficult. Both civilian and military water supplies are carefully monitored all the time to check for any increase in contamination, which might be caused naturally. These procedures would certainly be sufficient to detect well in advance any massive contamination and the standard water purification procedures would probably be sufficient to eliminate most of the danger in any case. To be effective the state of public hygiene would first have to be reduced to a very low level.

This does not mean, of course, that such attacks are never likely to be used. In the event of war, breakdowns in public standards of hygiene are almost to be expected. Furthermore, increasing centralization of food processing techniques, the advent of more rapid communications, and the increasing density of population centers have all tended to increase the risk of this kind of attack during the past 20 years. Such operations would not require large amounts of infective or toxic material. It has been estimated that anyone drinking 100 milliliters of water from a five million liter reservoir into which have been dropped five kilograms of partially purified botulinum toxin (Type A) would run a serious risk of poisoning. And, of course, the deliberate contamination of food or drink to eliminate important political or military personnel would be extremely difficult to prevent in the face of experienced saboteurs.

But all the available evidence points to the respiratory route of infection as the most effective means of disseminating a biological agent on a large scale. For one thing, this is often the most effective route in that many diseases can be caused by a smaller dose or produce more severe effects if the organisms concerned are inhaled rather than injected or ingested; anthrax caused by absorption of the organisms through the skin, for example, has a much lower mortality than does respiratory anthrax. Some people have also argued that this technique could be used to infect much larger populations for the disease would itself spread from man to man. It might therefore only be necessary to establish a small focus of infection in one corner of a country for the disease to spread eventually throughout the area of its own accord. This raises one of the most important questions about how biological agents should actually be used. Should they, regardless of whether they are spread by inhalation, injection, or ingestion, be designed to be epidemic, to spread themselves throughout a population? Certainly this is the popular idea of how a biological weapon would work. One way of doing this is through the introduction of animal vectors infected with disease and I have already explained the limitations of this technique. The alternative is to introduce a disease that will be spread directly from man to man. There are a number of reasons why this might be inadvisable.

For one thing, there is no way of calculating with any certainty what the results of such an attack will be. Epidemiology is an immensely complex subject and although —as I have indicated—certain theoretical advances have been made, the state of the art is still not very promising. This is mainly because the epidemiologist must either work theoretically or try to obtain data on past and present epidemics and then construct hypotheses to explain them. No experiments can be carried out on human populations and thus the normal techniques of science are denied to the epidemiologist. As a result there is no doctor or scientist alive today who could predict with absolute certainty the geographical spread or total deaths which might result from the introduction of an epidemic disease into a human population. He will certainly be in a position to take an informed guess—more informed for a rather limited number of diseases and much less informed for most others—but he would be the first to admit that his guesses could prove wildly wrong. The use of an epidemic disease will therefore introduce another important unknown into the already complex equations of biological warfare. Quite apart from the difficulties of using a weapon with unknown effects, there is also the danger that the disease could get completely out of hand and spread much further than originally anticipated. Under these circumstances it will be a foolhardy nation that first attempts to introduce an epidemic disease into a population as a military maneuver.

But more immediate and practical reasons are also involved. If the attacking force plans to occupy the region that has been subjected to biological warfare, it will have no option but to vaccinate every member of the attacking force against the disease. This assumes that a suitable vaccine is available—and if it is there is always the chance the enemy will have taken the precaution of vaccinating their troops or even civilians against the disease. More important, perhaps, is the fact that if a disease is epidemic it may have already occurred in that population and have been prevented from doing so by mass vaccination. This is an important point, for a microorganism can survive only if there is a suitable environment in which it can do so; if there is not, it will die out. Thus many of the diseases which are easily transmitted from man to man, such as smallpox, have already swept large areas of the world. In other areas, such as Europe and the United States, they have been prevented from gaining a substantial foothold by mass vaccination techniques. All this means that a highly epidemic agent may have less chance of infecting a population than a much rarer disease, which cannot be transmitted directly from one member of the population to another—and which is naturally rare for that very reason.

Any decision about using an epidemic agent will also involve the military objectives of the biological strike. If it is to strike down a sizable proportion of the population simultaneously—and thus allow the attacker to invade with much reduced resistance from the enemy—an epidemic agent will not be of great advantage over a nonepidemic one. As fast as some members of the population are immobilized by the disease, others will recover. The total effect will therefore be staggered when what is required is that a high proportion of the population be struck down simultaneously. Under such conditions it would be more efficient to use a large amount of infective material initially and to spread it as completely as possible over the area to be attacked. All those who succumb to the disease will then do so at once and, providing the agent is not directly transmissible, it will be possible to invade the territory shortly after the incubation period is over and with very little risk to the invader.

This method of attack will also put a much greater strain on the resources of the enemy. If no cure for the disease is known, he will be quite unable to protect his own troops and population. Nor will he have time to develop a protective vaccine against it if he does not already possess one. If, on the other hand, an epidemic agent were used it would be quite conceivable to develop and use a suitable vaccine between the first wave of infection and the second or third. Even if the disease could be treated with antibiotics, the simultaneous collapse of a large proportion of the population might place a much greater strain on antibiotic reserves than would a staggered incidence of disease. The conclusion seems fairly clear; the effects of a biological weapon must be assessed as those that result from primary casualties caused directly by the agent as it is delivered on to the battlefield; secondary infections will not help very much, will be difficult to control and might even spread to the attackers' own territory if the disease is epidemic. Of those diseases that are clearly being studied with great earnestness by biological warfare centers throughout the world, only a few are highly epidemic.

The fact that even some epidemic agents are now being studied as possible military agents gives considerable cause for alarm. One of the greatest dangers of biological warfare is that it is a potential weapon far from being completely understood. This, perhaps, would be somewhat less ominous if we knew that current plans were restricted to using agents incapable of producing epidemics. As I have explained, such agents are in any case more desirable from a military point of view. But perversely some of the epidemic diseases are caused by microorganisms that are far more suitable in other ways than are most of the non-epidemic agents. This is another example of the way in which the requirements of a biological agent can be, and often are, self-contradictory.

But we do know that when a biological agent is first used the object will be to cover the whole area to be attacked with infective material. Considerable research has been carried out into this aspect of infection and it has been shown that to be most effective the organisms should be suspended in a liquid that should be dispersed as an aerosol (many diseases are spread naturally in this way; a sneeze, for instance, liberates a highly infective aerosol spray). Fort Detrick has sponsored two conferences on this route of infection, and research there and elsewhere has shown that the size of aerosol particles should be between 1 and 5 microns in diameter (one micron is one ten-thousandth of a centimeter). Particles of this size will be small enough to pass down into the lung and to penetrate through the lung wall. Size is, in fact, quite critical; the dose of *Brucella suis* required to infect guinea pigs is 600 times greater with particles of 12 micron diameter than it is with particles of 1 micron diameter. The infective dose of Venezuelan equine encephalomyelitis increases by a factor of 14,000 if the particle's diameter is increased by a factor of 10.

Aerosols containing particles of 1-5 microns in diameter can be made by pressurizing the liquid containing the organisms and then releasing it through a small nozzle—just as paint, for instance, is released in a commercially available aerosol paint spray. But the liquid must be handled with great care—not subjected to heat, for instance, otherwise the organisms may be rapidly destroyed. Accurate figures of just what effect this pressurization of the liquid is likely to have are difficult to come by but one estimate suggests that a liquid containing 10^{10} viable organisms per milliliter before spraying is likely to contain about 10^9 viable organisms per milliliter immediately after spraying; in fact, this means that a good deal of the material is made useless but the initial concentrations are so high that the effect might not be very significant.

Aerosol particles of this size will drift down to earth—if released from a rocket, bomb, or aircraft—only slowly. A 0.5 micron particle, in still air, will take more than four days to fall only 10 feet. And if a 3-mile-an-hour wind were blowing, and the particle hit no obstacle, it would travel nearly 300 miles in that time. We do know that this is a successful technique at least on a small scale. Human volunteers have been infected with the organism that causes Q-fever at a distance of half a mile from where the agent was released. Guinea pigs have also been infected with a disease-causing organism 15 miles from the source. No doubt many more data are available to those working on such projects but I have seen no other figures published involving the spread of infectious and virulent aerosols. One of the reasons, of course, is that no government draws attention to any experiments it may conduct involving the release of infectious material, whether humans or guinea pigs are used as the experimental subjects.

Figures are available, however, on the spread of harmless organisms and of inanimate aerosols. Dr. LeRoy D. Fothergill, who has worked at Fort Detrick, has described how he released as an aerosol a 130 gallon suspension of the spore form of a harmless bacterium from the deck of a ship kept 2 miles from shore. The aerosol particles were between 1 and 5 microns in diameter and were subsequently found over an area extending 8 kilometers inland and 37 kilometers downwind. Throughout this area, even in buildings, anyone breathing unprotected would have inhaled more than 3,000 organisms in two hours. On another occasion he released 200 kilograms of zinc cadmium sulphide—a fluorescent material—as an aerosol of 2 micron diameter. The aerosol was released during a 250 kilometer boat trip, traveling 16 kilometers from the shore. The aerosol traveled 720 kilometers downwind and covered an area of nearly 90,000 square kilometers. In this area, the minimum inhaled dose was 15 particles a minute and the maximum was 15,000 particles a minute. These experiments proved conclusively what scientists had already expected: an aerosol cloud can be dispersed over great distances by the wind. Under appropriate meteorological conditions, they are likely to be distributed over an area far larger than the lethal area of even the largest nuclear weapon.

But it is at this stage in the use of biological weapons that the troubles really start. How stable will the organisms have to be to stand up to the rigors of exposure to the environment? Even before the environment begins to make its effects felt, the aerosol will start to lose its potency. For instance, the infective aerosol dose to guinea pigs of the tularemia organism is about 10-20 cells. But if the aerosol is left "standing" for 5½ hours, the dose will decrease to 150-200 cells (the infective dose to a human of a "fresh" tularemia aerosol is about 25 cells). This effect must be coupled with the additional destructive power of the environment. As the organisms drift down to earth —or are carried aloft by the prevailing winds—they will be subjected to variations in temperature and humidity and to radiation from the sun. These variations would be sufficient to kill many strains of microorganisms relatively quickly.

The temperature of the atmosphere at a height of

10,000 meters is about minus 60°C. Aerosol particles might be carried up to this height and down again several times during a lengthy dispersal under disturbed meteorological conditions; few organisms could withstand the resulting temperature variations. The only known possible exceptions are some of the viruses. At such a height, too, the intensity of ultraviolet radiation from the sun is much increased—there is far less atmosphere to absorb it—and this would be lethal to most bacteria and viruses. Furthermore, many bacteria are much more sensitive to sunlight at subzero temperatures. Any organisms which reached a height at which temperatures fell below freezing point and then returned to earth would be far less dangerous than they were when released.

The hazards at much lower levels of the atmosphere are also acute. Direct ultraviolet radiation from the sun is fairly lethal even at ground level and, unless they were released at night or during times of cloud cover, the microorganisms would suffer a heavy toll. Direct sunlight will kill most vegetative forms of bacteria in a matter of minutes and even spores in a few hours. Spores could be expected to survive the night and to live for days during overcast conditions. Vegetative forms might survive for 6-12 hours at night.

The atmosphere's humidity will also exert an important effect—although a less clear-cut one for some organisms survive better in wet conditions, some better in dry ones. It has been shown that 85 percent of a polio virus aerosol will remain viable for 23 hours (in the shade) if the humidity is 80 percent and the temperature 21-24°C. But at the same temperature and a humidity of 20-35 percent, only 1 percent of the aerosol will survive that time. On the other hand, the position is reversed for vaccinia virus which survives better in dry atmospheres.

The biological warfare centers of a number of countries have investigated the stability of viral and bacterial aerosols in some detail. Their conclusions obviously differ for each single organism but most of these studies show just how easily destroyed is a microorganism under these conditions. Doubtless some strains have been developed that could withstand the environmental hazards for at least some hours and under certain conditions. But the rigorous demands of stability must also have ruled out many strains that might otherwise have possessed nearly all the properties required of a biological weapon. Fort Detrick, in particular, is actively seeking ways of producing the organisms within a protective powder or within some form of protective coat. A good deal can be done, in fact, to improve the stability of a biological aerosol. The choice of the liquid used in the aerosol is critical and chemicals can be added to improve stability.

Theoretical calculations show that if about 100 milliliters of an aerosol containing 10^8 viable organisms per milliliter could be spread over an area of one square kilometer to a depth of two meters, anyone breathing the atmosphere for five minutes will inhale a dose of about 100 organisms. This would be more than an infective dose for some organisms. But such a calculation depends on two important factors. The first is that all the organisms remain viable—and that, as I have indicated, is a difficult requirement to fulfill. The second is that the aerosol is spread evenly over the square kilometer that constitutes the target. This is possibly an even more difficult requirement for it depends on yet other factors, which are quite outside human control—namely, the weather. Dust particles traveling at very high altitudes are believed to have been transported by the wind round the complete face of the globe. Smoke particles from forest fires in Canada have certainly been detected over the United Kingdom at a height of 10,000 meters and, even more relevant to the problem at hand, the spores of the crop disease known as rust have been transported by wind from Mexico to Canada. There would seem, then, to be little difficulty in using prevailing weather conditions to distribute infective aerosols over very wide areas. Indeed, the real problem may be distributing them so that they do not cover larger areas than are required—areas perhaps so large that they included neutral or friendly territory as well?

The dispersion of aerosols involves two quite different problems. The first is the spread of an agent over a local area—say a few kilometers square. The second is the spread of an agent over much larger areas, the kind of use Major General Marshall Stubbs, a former U.S. Army Chief Chemical Officer, was referring to when he said that biological agents exist that could be used to cause casualties in an area the width of a continent.

If the agent is to be dispersed locally, it will clearly have to be distributed during times of relative calm and when the light wind that does prevail is steady. Gusts or eddies might disperse the material—diluting it with uncontaminated air—before it had a chance to infect the enemy. Even a medium-strength wind blowing steadily would be difficult to use in this way. When a wind blows, the air speed is always much lower near ground level than it is higher up. This is because friction with the ground slows the wind down, just as friction with the shore bottom slows the underside of a breaking wave. This effect will also tend to dilute the aerosol cloud with fresh air because the air near ground level will become turbulent and aerosol and air will get thoroughly mixed. When using chemical weapons such an effect could jeopardize an attack but it is not likely to be so harmful to biological aerosols because they are so much more potent and so much less material is needed. Winds of about 4 miles per hour are thought ideal for chemical weapons and those of 10 miles per hour acceptable. When dispersing biological agents, higher wind speeds could be used; indeed the material should be made to travel fast so that it is exposed to the atmosphere for a minimum time—the shorter the time it is airborne, the more viable will it be. If the agent is not distributed directly above the target, it must of course be released upwind from the target. Such an observation may seem trivial but cases are on record of commanders trying to use tear gases to control riots and succeeding only in letting the chemicals blow back in the faces of the riot control troops. Such mistakes would be easy enough to make in war, particularly with a weapon as novel as a chemical or biological agent in the use of which, perhaps, the commanders had received only a minimum of training and their soldiers even less.

Horizontal winds are not the only ones that have to be considered when dispersing an aerosol. The atmosphere is continually moving vertically, mainly as a result of thermal currents. These occur during the day when the ground becomes heated and rising convection currents of air are produced. For this reason night would seem to be the best time for releasing aerosols, although the early morning and late afternoon are alternative possibilities; during these hours the atmosphere is said to be stagnant and the vertical motion of the air is stabilized, with a relatively low "ceiling" above which no mixing of air can occur. It is then that low lying mist can be seen hugging the ground and penetrating into every dip and valley. These are precisely the conditions that, coupled with a steady but slow wind, would be required for a local dispersion of chemical or biological weapons. They occur only during a portion of any day and far more commonly in some seasons than in others—during times when high pressure regions build up, for example. It follows that any areas in which the weather is highly variable—a characteristic for which the British Isles is infamous—are less prone to chemical and biological attack than other, more settled regions. But one must not make sweeping generalizations from these facts. Suffice to say that the commander of a chemical or biological task force will have to choose his time with care and probably wait for it with patience.

If a local attack is planned, the aerosol will have to be released at very low level. This can be a difficult operation in enemy territory as recent American experience in defoliation and crop destruction in Vietnam has shown. These operations are regarded by U.S. pilots as the most dangerous missions they have to fly. The aircraft is expected to be hit on any one mission and one aircraft in 1966 was hit on each of 28 successive missions. In these operations the Americans were spraying the chemicals more or less directly on the target from a height of a few hundred feet. Because they were treating relatively large areas—for chemical agents—they had no choice but to disperse the material with aircraft; bombs or missiles would not have given the even coverage over the area they wished to attack.

If a military concentration of personnel—or a civilian population—is to be attacked, many methods of dissemination are available. I have already mentioned the U.S. Sergeant missile, which was developed specially for delivering almost any kind of warhead, including chemical or biological material. How the warhead would actually be dispersed in the form of an aerosol is not public knowledge but presumably some pressure system would be incorporated which would either begin to function as the warhead neared the ground or would distribute the material after impact. The main difficulty here is that biological material must be released at low level otherwise the increased levels of ultraviolet radiation in the upper atmosphere will quickly kill off most of the agent. For that reason some form of bomb, with a parachute that opened at the right height, would seem an easier proposition—although if delivered during daylight it might give its presence away some time before the biological material could take effect.

It is difficult to write with insight about means of delivering biological agents because no nations have released any reliable information about such systems. Indeed, outside military circles, no one knows whether any nation does indeed possess a biological weapon that has reached the stage at which it would be militarily feasible to use it. Nearly all the reliable official statements about biological warfare have been concerned with defense. Stubbs' claim that biological agents exist capable of infecting areas as large as continents must also be interpreted with care. Probably all he meant was that the United States had the facilities to produce enough infectious material to infect theoretically an area of this size. This is a very different thing to the possession of a weapon which would actually work in practice with a near 100 percent chance of success and with militarily desirable results. Contamination of continent-sized areas would mean that the material had to be released at relatively high altitudes and the chances that it would survive sufficiently long to be transported in a viable condition from one end of even a small continent to the other are marginal to say the least. Nor do we have any reliable indication of where the material would end up. Of course some winds do blow steadily in a specified general direction during certain seasons. But, when planning a military operation designed to infect a continent, one would have to know with absolute certainty about the directions and strengths of winds over a huge area for a period of at least several days. At the moment we certainly do not have such information and the inherently changeable forms of most weather patterns suggest that we may never have.

By far the most controllable method of using a biological agent would be to spread it over the entire area to be attacked. In this way one would not have to rely on the aerosol being dispersed laterally by prevailing winds. To many scientists the idea of liberating a huge aerosol cloud along the windward edge of a large land mass and waiting for it to blow over the rest of the territory does not sound realistic. It would certainly be a dangerous operation, for there would always be a chance that the cloud might spread to regions other than the intended ones. From a military point of view it would probably be too unreliable a way of using what is in any case still an inherently unreliable and untested weapon.

But the difficulties of infecting a smaller area, say the size of a large city, are much less intense. This would not require a great deal of infective material and the chance of it spreading further than intended would be correspondingly reduced. The agent would not have to survive in the atmosphere for very long and so it would be more likely to remain in a viable condition for the time required. Furthermore, this small-scale release of biological aerosols has been proved effective in the simulated experiments which I have described. There are indications, too, that this kind of biological weapon is already available. Again, most of the evidence at our disposal comes from the United States.

A number of American military manuals make reference to the biological weapons which either are available or which could be made so. It is known that some military centers in the United States are concerned not with the research aspects of biological weapons but with their actual production. Plans have been made as to how such weapons might be used. But whether any of these weapons are at this minute actually filled with biological material is another matter. The answer is probably that they are not but this does not necessarily mean either that such weapons could not be made quickly available or that they have not reached the stage of development at which they could be used. As I have explained, it takes only a few days to grow sufficient infective material to contaminate large areas. Furthermore, we know that the properties of biological material tend to change on storage and so it would be preferable to keep a biological weapon in existence as a required strain in a laboratory rather than as an actual piece of hardware ready for use. Such strains are certainly available at a number of centers in the United States as well as, for example, at the M.R.E. in Porton in England. The difference, perhaps, is that plans have been finalized in the United States for using these strains as the starting material for biological weapons, which could be available within a matter of days. In Britain there is no public knowledge about similar plans and the emphasis is clearly that all work in this field is geared only to defense. If for any reason both countries had suddenly to produce and use biological weapons both could rise to the occasion: but the United States could certainly do it more quickly and her machinery for effecting the biological attack would work more smoothly for it has been planned in advance. We know, for instance, that if the United States used a lethal biological agent it would be one thought capable of killing between 25 and 50 percent of the population attacked. If an incapacitating disease is used, it is expected to put 25 to 30 percent of the population out of action.

We know also that the United States has a very large testing ground at Dugway in Utah. This is an important point for before any biological weapon is used it must be tested. To what extent biological weapons have been tested at Dugway is not known but it seems doubtful that any large-scale test can have been made with highly infectious material because of the danger of the material affecting nearby populations. Indeed, it is difficult to see how any biological weapon can be effectively tried out before it is used on a real enemy. This has two rather frightening implications. The first is that a nation such as the United States or, and this is perhaps much more likely, a smaller nation will be tempted to try out a biological weapon on a real enemy simply as a means of perfecting a weapon system currently of unproven value. I do not need to emphasize that experiments on human populations involving infectious material are to be avoided; they are as likely to lead to epidemics or other unwanted side effects as they are to perfect a new weapons system. The second implication is that when biological weapons are first used that action may be as much experimental as it is strategic or tactical. If there are moral doubts about whether or not biological weapons are a legitimate means of waging war in any case, there must surely be even further objections to experimenting with them on human populations. Thus the fact that biological weapons are so far of unproven military value and suspected of being unreliable affords us little comfort. It means that the temptation to test them on humans is that much stronger.

CHAPTER 7

"Only We Can Prevent Forests"

Five million gallons of herbicides and defoliants have been purchased at a cost of $32 million for use in Vietnam during the fiscal year 1967 . . . We're told these substances "do not sterilise the soil, are harmless to human and animal life." I'm afraid this can only bring a hollow laugh from any ecologist.

Peter Scott, 1967

THE IDEA of using chemical or biological weapons against the crops or animals on which we depend is no fantasy. As I write this chapter American forces are spraying the crops of the Vietnamese with weed-killers. By the end of 1966 they had destroyed some 150,000 acres of rice paddy fields. This is an activity which has caused strong moral objections to be raised not so much because the technique used is a form of chemical warfare but for other reasons. Crop destruction, whether by flamethrower, incendiary bomb, weed-killer, or biological warfare, is an invidious method of waging war. In underdeveloped areas such as Southeast Asia it is particularly invidious for there many people are at least ill-nourished if not actually underfed. If food is made even scarcer by the war machine, it is the weakest members of the population that suffer first—women, particularly pregnant ones, young children, elderly people, and anyone who is not in full health. Crop destruction is a discriminate means of waging war—it discriminates in favor of what should be the prime target, the combatants, and instead selects for its victims those who are not most fully involved in the battle. And starvation is a long and ugly death. Yet this form of chemical warfare, the only one being extensively practiced at the present time, has apparently been condoned by most of the world. Indeed it has gone largely unnoticed and, when it has been reported, it has been dealt with in only a superficial manner.

The reasons are perhaps not hard to find. We live in a world accustomed to half the population being underfed. Indeed, some people see the fact that half the world population is underfed as being some kind of natural means of postponing the disaster with which we are continually threatened by the population explosion. In the face of such opinion it is perhaps not so amazing that we allow crops to be destroyed, in an already starving world, for the sake of political controversy.

In this chapter we shall be concerned with the possibilities of using chemical and biological weapons against crops and animals on an even larger scale. Ultimately, of course, we depend very heavily on domestic animals and crops—not just for food, but for a host of other raw materials, such as cotton, wood, leather, and some pharmaceuticals, and other commodities which chemists are not yet able to synthesize without the help of living organisms.

There are plenty of historical examples that indicate that the diseases of crops can have profound effects on man. The Irish potato famine of the 1840s, for instance, completely wrecked that country's economy and had widespread repercussions on many aspects of Irish life. (Half a million people are said to have died as a result of the famine and 1½ million to have emigrated.) Had the Irish been waging war at that time, the potato blight fungus, which did all the damage, would have had a serious effect on the country's ability to carry on the struggle. In 1943 another fungus completely ruined more than 90 percent of India's rice crop. Had it not proved possible to divert grain to India, the effects would have been even greater than they were. But how easy would it be to duplicate these effects artificially, against the improved methods of disease control, which have come into being since the last war?

First we should consider the range of crops whose destruction might produce the intended effect. Ideally, of course, they would have to be staple crops. In most of the world this means cereals (such as wheat, corn, and barley or rice), with potatoes in third place but having less importance. It would not be difficult to live without the other, less important crops such as brussels sprouts, coffee, turnips, or melons. Their destruction would at most present only a minor nuisance. Of course, if some organism could be developed that would destroy the lot—or at least a high proportion of them—the effect would be much greater. Fortunately, although some viruses attack quite wide ranges of plant species, no pathogen is yet known that would spread rapidly through many different kinds of crops, and the chance that one will be developed is very small. The economy of some small isolated community that depended for its economic survival entirely on one crop, such as sugar cane, might be ruined by the introduction of some suitable pest or disease. But most large nations have much more effective means of overcoming smaller ones and they would be unlikely to risk the censorship of world opinion to achieve an end which could be attained more quickly and more reliably by other means.

This brings us back to cereals. Rice is the staple food of more than 75 percent of Asian countries. It is also a crop to which a good deal of military attention has already been turned. For example, Elinor Langer has reported that the highest award the U.S. Army can give to civilians, the Distinguished Service Medal, was recently awarded to a research scientist at Fort Detrick for work on development of a rice blast fungus—the cause of a disease that has repeatedly damaged Asian rice crops.

Cereals now constitute about three-quarters of the world's food. Even with today's techniques of pest and disease control—which are applied less systematically to rice than to other cereals—losses from disease are enormous. In the Soviet Union the outcome of the annual grain harvest is awaited anxiously from year to year because imported grain has to be kept to a minimum; if the harvest fails it means invariably that the population will go short of bread. In some countries, harvest failures are less serious for they mean simply that more grain must be transported from other regions where the harvest has been better and where there is an excess. The same free trading facilities might not exist in war, however, in which case the outcome of the harvest might be of greater consequence.

Cereals can be attacked by both chemical and biological means on a scale that is not possible with any other technique. Which weapon is likely to be used would depend very much on the other conditions prevailing. For instance, the Americans have chosen chemical techniques of crop destruction in Vietnam for a very simple reason. They wish to attack relatively small areas—those on which they believe the Vietcong depend for their food. Furthermore these areas lie within country that is not powerfully defended with sophisticated radar systems and antiaircraft guns or missiles. This means that they can get their planes in over the crops at low level, and simply spray them with herbicide. The amount of herbicide used on these relatively small areas is large but not impossibly so. The advantage of the technique is that the chemical works quickly and reliably.

But if the object were to treat a very large area of crops, the expense of the chemical, and the difficulty of applying it, would simply be too great. Here a biological agent would be better for much less material would have to be used, provided that the agent was able to multiply and spread itself throughout the crop. There clearly would be disadvantages for biological agents are not so reliable as chemical ones and this use of them has not so far been proved in war; furthermore, the degree to which they spread would depend heavily on the season. We can expect them to suffer from the same disadvantages as those biological weapons which might be used against man but with one difference: they would be selected for their epidemic effect and might therefore be more likely to get out of control. The other occasion on which it might seem tempting to use anticrop biological weapons would be where it was needed to destroy a small area of crops lying within well-defended territory. This might also require the use of an infective agent; planes would not be able to fly over the area and an agent that spread itself would have to be used.

We know that in the United States at least serious consideration is being given to the use of chemical and biological weapons against crops. Several of the contracts, which have been awarded to universities, colleges, and industry, involve studies of the possible effects of these agents on different crops in different parts of the world. For example, Research Analysis Corporation, a small firm outside Washington, has produced a brochure boasting of the following "research capabilities": studies of biological and chemical attacks on crops and some analysis of effects on livestock; covert attack on a food crop; and impact of a chemical attack on guerrilla food crops. These are all studies which the firm has undertaken under government contract. How would they be effected in practice?

To military thinkers who are trying to exploit biological weapons it must sometimes seem that nature really is working against them. This applies particularly to crop pathogens, for two quite distinct characteristics are required: the pathogen must be airborne and it must be viable under all the varied weather conditions it is likely to encounter. There are many stable pathogens—most of the fungi form hardy spores—and there are many airborne pathogens. But for some reason, or perhaps by chance, those that can be disseminated, or which disseminate themselves with the help of the wind, are generally extremely sensitive to weather conditions. The stable pathogens are usually those that remain in the soil and spread only slowly. The critical dependency of crop pathogens on favorable weather is shown by the annual variations of total crop production. These variations are mostly due to weather conditions affecting the pathogens, either preventing them from spreading or enabling them to do so.

The selection of a suitable agent is likely to be made that much more difficult by the fact that some crops are routinely sprayed with an appropriate fungicide wherever the weather favors the spread of an important pathogen. This is an effective, if costly, means of keeping disease at bay and, of course, commercial fungicides cannot distinguish pathogens that are naturally occurring from those which have been artificially introduced. The fungicide would destroy both with equal rapidity. But in some areas crop strains have been developed that are resistant to certain diseases and which therefore do not require spraying with fungicide. It is in these areas, as we shall see, that biological weapons might be used to their greatest effect.

Perhaps the most serious cereal diseases are the rusts, and particularly black (stem) rust. This disease can spread rapidly under favorable conditions. Even today it still causes millions of pounds worth of damage every year, in spite of the immense effort that has been put into finding and developing new varieties of wheat that resist the local forms of the fungus. But, it seems, as fast as new strains are developed, which are resistant to the local form of the fungus, new strains of fungus spring up able to attack the new varieties. One strain of the fungus, first noted in 1953, which attacks oats, had still not been satisfactorily defeated in 1966. It was regularly destroying some 6 percent of the U.S. oat crop every year. To find a solution an Israeli scientist, who reasoned that some wild forms of cereal had survived all forms of the fungus in the Middle East for many thousands of years, collected 2,350 different samples of wild cereals and tested them for resistance to 264 strains of the rust fungus; a strain of wild oats, found growing near Mount Carmel, turned out to be the most resistant. It is hoped that when it has been further developed it will save the U.S. farmer up to $26 million a year. And to prepare for further developments of new strains of rust, new varieties of wheat and barley are now being tested, and will go into use when a new strain of rust strikes.

All this is splendid for agriculture and may mean—as it has already in some parts of the world—that fungicides can be dispensed with altogether or used only very occasionally. It is in such conditions that a biological agent might prove most effective. A new strain of the black (stem) rust fungus of wheat, for instance, could do a great deal of damage if its spores were released in large numbers over a wide area. It is also more stable than most airborne fungi, which are relatively stable.

There is also the possibility that crops might be attacked by a form of pathogen which, though well known elsewhere, had never before been found in that particular region. Here there is almost an analogy with the smallpox situation I have already mentioned; agricultural authorities now take just as much precaution to ensure that foreign animal and plant diseases are not introduced into their countries as public health authorities do to ensure that human diseases are not introduced. The spread of one of these plant diseases, which was completely new to a territory, might have quite severe results. It is as well to remember what happened when maize rust, which had long been known in America, was introduced to Africa. In a relatively short time it lowered African maize production so much that some countries previously exporters of maize were turned into importers.

The U.S. Agricultural Research Service has produced a special pamphlet on the subject of protection of crops and animals against attack by biological warfare. In this it is made clear that the problem is regarded as a serious one, that the deliberate spread of pests as well as diseases is to be feared, and that one of the principal dangers is from new diseases or pests, which were either previously unknown in the United States or which had been eradicated from that country. During 1961 alone, nearly 324,000 samples of unauthorized plant material were prevented from being imported in the United States by officials at the ports of entry. More than half was found in travelers' baggage. Also intercepted were thousands of plant pests which, if they had been allowed to spread and succeeded in so doing, might have done great damage.

The same pamphlet points to the particular dangers to which American crops might be exposed. The Khapra beetle, one of the world's worst stored-grain pests, is one of these. It was first found on the West Coast in 1953 and spread to more than 700 storage buildings in the next seven years. The beetle was still a potential threat in 1961 although fumigation to destroy it had cost the nation more than $5 million. The report also points to witchweed, stem rust, the Mediterranean fruit fly, and the white leaf virus of rice, among others, as pests and diseases that have at one time or another threatened U.S. crops. Five species of potato weevil and the Asiatic rice borer are given as examples of pests that have never established themselves in the States. Considered in the long term, these are clearly very real threats to agriculture but are much more likely to be accidentally introduced in the United States than deliberately. They are not the kind of pests with which one might win a war, for their rate of multiplication and destruction is slow even on the biological scale.

The slow spread of many biological agents is not their only disadvantage. Like the organisms that produce human disease, they are no respecters of national boundaries. And this is an even more important consideration in biological warfare against crops than it is against men. The reason is that the plant diseases used would have to be relied upon to spread themselves in an epidemic manner. As I have explained this is a procedure which involves so many unknowns that it would probably be rigorously avoided when spreading human diseases. If it is to be rigorously adopted when spreading plant diseases then one must expect extremely variable results. The attack might have no effect. On the other hand, both sides might end up with an acute food shortage and a serious disease eradication program on their hands. Clearly, it is advisable to use chemicals in preference wherever possible.

The chemical weapons that have been developed for use against man are of very real military value. The chemical weapons for use against plants are older, more thoroughly tested, and have reached an even higher degree of sophistication. In the form of insecticides and herbicides, they are both effective and potent. It must certainly be significant that the Americans chose chemicals rather than biological weapons in their attack on the Vietnamese jungle and paddy field. There is a host of compounds to choose from, all cheaply mass produced by industry.

Among the most effective of these are a family of chemicals that rely for their effect on a biological action. These are the so-called growth hormones. Unlike the bacteria and viruses—many of which can attack only a few or a single crop species—they are effective against the complete range of broad-leaved plants. The two most well known are 2,4-D (2,4-dichlorophenoxyacetic acid) and 2,4,5-T (2,4,5-trichlorophenoxyacetic acid), which are sprayed at a concentration of around half a pound per acre. These chemicals are prepared synthetically by the chemical industry and rely for their effect on augmenting the growth of a plant to such an extent that it burns itself out within a few days.

These chemicals, and a powerful desiccant called cacodylic acid, have been used in large quantities. During the year ended July 1, 1966, $10 million worth of herbicides and defoliants was purchased from industry by the government for use in Vietnam. Next year five million gallons were used, worth $32 million, and for the year ending July 1, 1968, $50 million worth have been ordered. By early 1967 American forces had destroyed

150,000 acres of crops and defoliated 500,000 acres of jungle. In spite of almost too ready assurances by the Department of Defense that the chemicals are completely harmless to mammals, some scientists are worried about the possibilities of a build-up of chemical contamination in underground water supplies. Ecologists have more to worry about, however. When the jungle is sprayed with these chemicals, the leaves on the trees turn brown within about four days and eventually drop off. If the dose has been large, the tree will die within weeks. One dead tree is of little import. But an area of dead forest is another matter. Such an action is bound to have a serious effect on the ecology of the region and one that could prove to be irreversible. Scientists, at least, are seriously worried about the possibilities of soil erosion resulting from the Vietnamese defoliation operations. Clearly the pilots who carry out these operations are not so worried. Hung up in their headquarters is their motto—the title of this chapter: "Only we can prevent forests."

Fortunately, perhaps, we are not likely to see an escalation of the use of chemicals to destroy crops. The main reason is that dissemination is extremely difficult, even in an underdeveloped region such as Vietnam. The planes required must be slow, heavily built transport aircraft. The American forces are using C-123 Provider planes which were officially designed as troop carriers—each aircraft carrying up to 60 passengers. In 1967 a flight of 16 of these aircraft was in constant use and the operation had been in progress more than two years. The oldest plane was hit by ground fire more than 500 times and several pilots earned casualty medals—known as Purple Hearts —more than once. When the pilots, ironically known as "Ranchers," earn three Purple Hearts they are sent home.

The planes can release nearly 900 gallons of defoliant

in a single four-minute run—sufficient to treat about 250 acres of ground at a cost, in defoliant alone, of nearly £2,000. In 1965, more than 500 of these flights were made, destroying an estimated 75,000 acres of crops and defoliating 100,000 acres of forest. In July 1965 more than 90,000 gallons of defoliating chemicals were used in 137 missions.

The fact that the aircraft are hit so frequently—more often than not—is not surprising. They must cruise at a speed of 130 knots at a height of 150 feet over long distances. In any country where antiaircraft defense was more sophisticated, these aircraft would have little chance of returning to base in one piece. Only in a slow moving war in underdeveloped territory is this kind of operation possible and the French, who practiced it in Algeria, found it equally difficult. It is one of those perverse facts of strategy that operations of this kind are possible only over underdeveloped countries where the population is largely agricultural and where food is already scarce.

So far I have discussed the possible uses of chemical and biological weapons against crops. An alternative target which might have a severe effect on the supplies of food and many other natural products are domesticated animals. American military forces rely for 40 percent of their rations on American livestock and any radical decrease in the quantities available for slaughter would surely have an effect on the civilian standard of living if not on the efficiency of the military machine. A biological attack on livestock would have other costly results. Between 1902 and 1922 foot and mouth disease caused 325,000 domestic animals to be slaughtered in the United States, at an estimated cost of $390 million. It is estimated that a serious outbreak of this disease now would cost nearer $500 million. In some parts of the world, where traction still relies heavily on animals such as oxen, the effects might be even more severe, cutting down the supplies of animal food and removing the means of caring for and perhaps irrigating the land, which provided the alternative plant foods.

As far as I know there are no plans or even prospects of using chemical attacks against animals. However, detailed thought has been given to the potential of biological agents. And here we are no longer quite so much in the dark as when considering biological warfare against man. It has been practiced, though not during war, against animals and with great effect. The best example is the deliberate spread of myxomatosis. This illustrates the potentialities and difficulties of biological warfare so well that I shall deal with it in some detail.

The rabbit is a fast reproducer. In three years, one pair could, in theory, give rise to several million descendants. In the 1940s the 500-million-strong rabbit population of Australia which far outnumbered the human inhabitants, was causing an annual loss of more than £100 million. In 1950 the Australians introduced myxomatosis, a virus disease. The effect was sensational. Within months of the release of the virus, 90 percent of the rabbit population was dead. The same story was repeated in other parts of the world. In May 1952, one or two rabbits were inoculated with the virus in the department of Eure et Loire in France. By the end of 1953 the disease had spread through 26 departments in France and through Holland, Germany, Belgium, and Switzerland, killing between 60 and 90 percent of the population. The rabbits could take no evasive action and they were completely unprotected against the disease. If a similar virus existed that could be used on a human population, it is difficult to tell what the result would be. One must remember, however, that we could have treated the disease to some extent and that we have powerful techniques for preventing disease from spreading—if not between towns then at least across real geographical barriers. The fact that biological warfare against rabbits has been proved efficient and practical does not necessarily mean that the same is true of biological warfare against humans. I shall return to this point later in the chapter.

But since the 1950s both the virus and the rabbit population have changed. Australia's rabbit population has doubled again in the past few years and in 1967 was estimated at about 100 million. New strains of myxomatosis virus seem to have little effect. The reason is thought to be that most rabbits have been immunized by a relatively harmless virus that gives protection to the rabbits against the more virulent strains. The Australians have been experimenting with chemical warfare against the rabbits and have come up against just the kind of difficulty I was discussing in relation to Vietnam. They have dropped diced carrots spiced with a new poison which, in some areas, has killed up to 90 percent of the rabbit population. But only in those areas where the food was actually dropped. As these were virtually insignificant compared to the vast areas of land which the rabbit inhabits, the overall effect has been small.

Australian scientists are now planning to find a way to overcome the myxomatosis barrier. They have tried to find a new carrier for the disease and had 12,000 European fleas shipped from Europe for that purpose. Only nine survived the journey. These were carefully bred until a population of 100 was reached. Then the building in which they lived was accidentally sprayed with insecticide and they all died. There could be no better example of the difficulties surrounding attempts to use biological war-

fare techniques, which involve the spread of insect vectors.

But the fact remains that myxomatosis was spread
among the rabbit population with great success. If rabbits,
why not horses, cows, sheep, or even oxen? In some ways,
and in some countries, the livestock population represents
a greater hazard than do crops. In the United States, for
instance, there are often huge agricultural surpluses, particularly of grain. But there is no such surplus of livestock
and a biological attack causing widespread disease might
have a serious effect on the supply of protein or natural
products much more quickly.

There is a wide choice of diseases that might provide
possible antianimal biological agents. Among the viruses,
for instance, are those that cause foot and mouth, fowl
plague, Newcastle disease, and African swine fever. The
foot and mouth virus is one of the most infectious known.
It is thought to reduce animal productivity by as much as
25 percent every year. In the United Kingdom, policy is
still to eradicate the disease completely. This is a costly
procedure for it means that all the animals likely to have
come into contact with it—and this includes cows, sheep,
goats, and pigs—must be slaughtered. Even the relatively
minor outbreak that occurred in the north of England at
the end of 1966 caused 45,000 animals to be slaughtered.

At least 40 different antigenic strains of the foot and
mouth virus are known, and there are probably many more
yet to be discovered. They can survive for periods of 15
weeks or more in hay and straw or on wood, and are
thought to be outstanding among the viruses for their
survival capacity. Nevertheless, warm, sunny weather
greatly decreases their survival time and this may explain
why outbreaks are more common in cold, damp weather.
But the virus is tougher than most microorganisms. Good

vaccines are available against many strains but there are so many of them that identification of the particular one involved and preparation of the appropriate vaccine is a laborious procedure.

Newcastle disease of poultry, on the other hand, presents a smaller risk because the methods of dealing with outbreaks are different. A simple and effective vaccine is available, which can be administered by the ordinary farm worker. Many countries have now changed from a complete eradication/slaughter policy to a vaccination procedure because of the great costs of the former. This has a double advantage in that the animals build up resistance against the disease, either naturally or artificially, because it is almost invariably present somewhere. But where eradication procedures are used, the animals have very low resistance as they never come into contact with it. If the disease does establish itself, they are likely to be as susceptible to it as the rabbit was found to be to myxomatosis; the effects can be equally disastrous for the animal population.

The livestock in the United Kingdom are worth around £1,000 million. This is a large sum but, by the standards of international conflict and the expense it involves, it is by no means huge. And a biological attack on livestock could be expected, even if spectacularly successful, to knock out only a small proportion of the total. Is the target a worthwhile one and would such an attack add much power to the arm of an aggressor intent on winning a war? It seems unlikely. The countries which depend to a great extent on livestock have already shown that they are capable of struggling on in the face of quite appallingly high incidences of animal disease. The world as a whole loses about £1,000 million worth of livestock every year to animal disease. In Europe, 15 percent of livestock succumb to disease, or have to be slaughtered, every year. A biological attack, if successful, might double this percentage but the effect would surely not be very great in the terms of an international or global war. To be sure, there are more limited uses for antianimal biological agents in local actions, which are conducted on a much smaller scale, particularly where, as in some underdeveloped areas, livestock are still used for traction. In a cold war situation, where the time scale of events was slow, such an attack might produce a serious effect on a small population. It might also have a serious effect on the availability of manpower. In the Soviet Union, where the problem has been analyzed in some depth, it has been estimated that seven men would be required to tend every hundred head of cattle in the event of a biological attack against livestock.

There is another aspect, however, which merits even more serious consideration. There are a number of bacterial diseases that affect both livestock and man. And these diseases are among those that might be considered useful agents in a biological action in which man was the principal target.

One of the most important of these is brucellosis, otherwise known as Malta fever or undulant fever. It is produced, as I have said, by three different species of bacteria, one of which infects goats, one which infects cattle, and one which infects pigs. These bacteria are relatively stable and can live in unpasteurized milk, for instance, for several weeks or in the soil, if dry, for up to two months. The disease is passed to man when he eats contaminated food, when he inhales the bacteria, or when the bacteria pass through broken skin. Those in frequent contact with infected animals are, of course, at the greatest risk and in the Soviet Union some of them are protected by vaccine. In man the symptoms are those of a slowly mounting fever, which may be severely incapacitating but which has a low mortality rate.

Another of the diseases common to both man and livestock is anthrax, often known as woolsorter's disease, since it is easily contracted by those who come into frequent contact with untreated wool. If the bacterium is inhaled the disease is severe and the result normally fatal. If absorbed through the skin, the effects are much more mild. As I have mentioned, this is a disease caused by a spore-forming bacterium and it can infect cows, sheep, goats, and pigs. It is very infective and because of the stability of the spores difficult to eliminate once firmly established. It is transmitted from man to man only rarely and this, of course, is an advantage if used as a biological weapon. The symptoms are rather diverse, which means that it is difficult to detect; so although it can be treated with antibiotics, if caught in time, the respiratory form is often fatal.

A third disease I should mention is glanders—the one the Germans were accused of trying to propagate in horses in World War I. This disease is found in horses, mules, and donkeys and can be transmitted to man. The disease is serious, usually fatal, and forms deep ulcers, material from which is highly infective. Because it is so often fatal there is little immunity to the disease. One factor that might tell against the use of this disease is that it is much more serious if it is caused by bacteria penetrating the skin; the respiratory form, which does also occur, is less severe and recovery is more common. Here there is a clear need for a nation developing the disease as a biological weapon to find a strain that is particularly harmful when infective through the respiratory route.

There are other diseases common to both man and animals but the three I have described are among the most likely contenders for use in biological warfare. I doubt that they would ever be used to attack animals alone for man makes a better military target. But the fact that they do infect both cattle and man might give them a real advantage over agents which attack only animals and a minor advantage over agents that attack only man. Even so, if there were satisfactory agents available to attack man alone, they would probably be used. But as far as anyone not actually involved in research on biological warfare can tell, anthrax and glanders, at least, seem to be among the best biological agents. The fact that they might also produce severe effects on livestock populations is simply another advantage in their favor.

Earlier in this book I mentioned that biological warfare has been used for decades in man's perpetual battle against the pests that threaten our crops. I would like to consider some examples of these biological battles in a little more detail because they shed some light not only on biological warfare against crops and livestock but also on the nature of the difficulties involved in any form of biological warfare. But first I should point out an important difference. Most uses of biological control have relied not on insect diseases but on importing competitors or predators of the insects doing the damage. This need not worry us too much, however, for the principles are the same: exploiting populations of living organisms—be they viruses, bacteria, or insects—to work in a rather specified way over a large area.

Perhaps the best known success story of biological control concerns the prickly pear—a form of cactus already out of hand in Australia by the turn of the century and which then occupied about 10 million acres of good land. By 1925 it occupied 60 million acres, about half of which was impenetrable to man. It was in this year that 2,750 eggs of the *Cactoblastis* moth were imported, in the hope that the moth would multiply so rapidly that it would reduce the level of its food supply—the prickly pear—by huge amounts. Ten years later the prickly pear had virtually been eaten away. But this success was the exact opposite of what would have been expected from theory: it had always been thought that an insect would not reduce its food supply beyond the point where its own population would suffer. This is a good example of how wrong predictions about the use of a biological agent can be. In the case of the prickly pear, the effect was all to the good; in biological warfare it might mean global disaster.

Writing in *Science Journal* (April 1965), Sir Vincent B. Wigglesworth dwelt on this point at some length: "Operations of this sort can have far reaching and sometimes unforeseen effects. After the Australian success *Cactoblastis* was introduced into South Africa. It was successful up to a point in eradicating the prickly pear but, after a time, it reached a point of equilibrium with far too much prickly pear remaining. The cochineal insect, *Dactylopius opuntiae*, was therefore introduced from Australia to supplement the effects of *Cactoblastis*. It proved highly effective. However, farmers in South Africa have plantations of spineless cactus which is used for feeding stock, and *Dactylopius* soon spread to these plantations where it caused much damage, and insecticidal methods had to be devised to control it. Furthermore, there is in South Africa a ladybird *Exochomus* which has proved extremely useful in the biological control of woolly aphis, mealy bugs and other Coccid pests of citrus and vines. *Exochomus* soon recognized an attractive prey in the cochineal insects on the prickly pears and worked havoc among the weed controlling agent." These are the sort of ecological problems, often unexpected, which result from the use of biological agents. There is no reason to believe that they might not also result from the use of biological warfare proper.

One of the most important diseases to have been used against inspect pests is known as milky disease. It affects the Japanese beetle *Popillia,* which can severely damage lawns and pasture. The disease is caused by a spore-forming bacterium. These bacteria have been collected from infected grubs, injected into the ground and the disease has spread among the beetles, bringing them under control. Another bacterium, *Bacillus thuringiensis,* has been used to control caterpillars that defoliate the forests of southern France. Here the analogy is closer, for the bacteria were grown in laboratory culture and then sprayed over the forest.

It has been estimated that two out of every three attempts to use biological control against crop pests have been entirely unsuccessful. The successful examples I have quoted have been far outnumbered by failures and biological control has been frowned on by agriculturists ever since it failed to live up to its early promise at the turn of the century. But, one might ask, if it does work one time out of three, and if we can compare these results with those from biological warfare, would this not be sufficient to provide a useful weapon? Let me make it quite clear that the analogy between biological warfare and biological control of crop pests is a tenuous one. But it does have some purpose: it sets a ceiling to what might reasonably be achieved with present-day technology. There is no reason to think that biological weapons could be used successfully against man with a better than one in three chance, without some large advance in our knowledge of microbiology and public health. And there are reasons to believe that the "success" rate would be a good deal lower.

First, insect pests can take no evasive action. Biological weapons can be countered to some extent by good public hygiene, vaccination, antibiotics, and many other techniques. Secondly, we cannot experiment with biological weapons in the sense that we can with biological control. This again would tend to lower the success rate. Third, there would be many military situations in which the time scales involved in biological control—sometimes months, more often years—would be far too long. A study of the success of biological control does not prove that biological warfare can never be successful. It simply confirms what can be deduced in other ways: that it might be useful in local wars, that it might be effective once in every several attempts and that in those several attempts one can expect to produce some unexpected results. This does not add up to a compelling specification for a weapon system.

CHAPTER 8

Toward the Toxic Club

> It is my hope that through this use of incapacitating
> agents the free world will have a relatively cheap and rapid
> means of both fighting and deterring limited war which has
> come to the forefront in the international political scene
> in the last several years.
>
> Major General Marshall Stubbs,
> former U.S. Army Chief Chemical Officer

CHEMICAL and biological agents must surely be the most
flexible weapon systems ever invented. The rifle is limited to killing individuals, the machine gun to killing small
groups, high explosive bombs to killing large groups,
and nuclear weapons to causing massive destruction of
both property and life. For a start, toxic weapons do not
necessarily kill. And although neither chemical nor biological weapons will have any effect on property they could
be used in place of almost any other weapon. They might
be used to kill a national leader or to threaten an entire
continent. The task of discussing their military roles is
therefore equivalent to a thesis on the uses of nearly all the
military weapons which have ever been invented. For
that reason, and because detailed information about the
capabilities of biological weapons has never been released, we shall be able only to skim the surface of the
military uses of toxic weapons. What can be done in more

158

detail, however, is to examine their role in current political and military thinking. In many ways this is a subject of greater importance for the chemical and biological armory promises to change our thinking about the uses and objectives of war. And as war is but an instrument of international negotiation—admittedly an extreme one—these weapons could prove to have a decisive role to play in the evolution of national power and the way in which future conflicts may be settled.

Since World War II the major nations have been locked in a struggle known as the cold war. At times over the past twenty years this war has become alternately colder and warmer. With the emergence of fundamental differences between China and the Soviet Union there have been signs of a thaw in the Soviet-American dispute; equally there have been signs of a freezing in relations between China and the West, and the promise of other limited struggles with that country in the future.

Perversely, the invention of nuclear weapons is probably partly responsible for the fact that no major war has broken out since 1945. The major nations, to use the cliché, have been locked in a state of nuclear equipoise. Both sides have built up such huge stockpiles of nuclear devices that all-out nuclear war between them has become unthinkable. Each side realizes that, if it started a war in which nuclear weapons of any size were used, the results would be so devastating that neither side could expect to gain. On the contrary it could expect to lose almost everything. But, to consider every eventuality, we should ask if toxic weapons have any role to play if all-out nuclear war ever is begun.

The one area in which they may prove of military use stems from the immense destructive power of nuclear weapons. Nuclear weapons can be used to attack both people and sites—military or industrial ones—of major importance. Sometimes these functions are not synonymous. For instance, if a plan were made to knock out a major proportion of missile sites in the United States with nuclear weapons, the population toll would be relatively small. Missile sites are placed some distance away from population centers. But this would be a rather limited objective for such an extreme action as nuclear attack. If nuclear weapons are ever used, the objective of the mission in which they are involved will probably be much broader; at the least, it will involve massive attacks on civilian populations. This was the reason for the great concern about the construction of nuclear shelters during the past decade. So presumably nuclear weapons would also be directed at major population centers.

Such an attack would inevitably destroy the essence of civilization—it would knock out major industries, power stations, bridges, and railways. This, of course, is one reason why nuclear war has so far been rigorously avoided. There is little advantage to be gained from destroying a nation to this extent; it leaves nothing for the victor to win, even if he himself survives the nuclear retaliation which, we are told, is likely to occur within the quantum of the nuclear time scale—four minutes.

In other words, the fact that nuclear weapons so readily destroy property is one of the main deterrents to their use. Unhappily, the coming of age of chemical and biological weapons may provide an alternative. These are weapons that leave property totally undamaged. In a sense, then, they form a complementary offensive weapon to nuclear power. They might make possible a nuclear war which could be fought to win and in which the victor could take over the country he had quelled in a relatively unchanged condition. The nuclear armory would be used to eliminate the enemy's offensive capability and the toxic armory would be used for massive destruction of the human population. This is not a happy picture. Having learned—almost—to live with nuclear weapons, we can see a technical development that might make nuclear war a conceivable proposition. It could invalidate 20 years of hard and rewarding work at the disarmament conferences.

Of course, the argument I have just used involves hundreds of other factors—such as the nature of the conflict, the size of nuclear stockpiles, and the desirability of enemy property—which I have not even mentioned. It may well be that the type of nuclear/toxic attack I have described ranks very low as far as military probability is concerned. I hope it does. But so much is at stake here that it is a point worth remembering.

But if the probability is low that we shall ever use toxic and nuclear weapons together, it is certainly a good deal higher that we shall use toxic weapons without nuclear ones. Indeed, there is a possibility that toxic weapons—for certain countries and in certain situations—could become a substitute for nuclear weapons. They provide a means of achieving nuclear results without a nuclear holocaust. The sort of action I have in mind is one in which the aim is to kill or incapacitate millions of people but to leave the country otherwise unharmed.

The large-scale toxic attack is the one that figures most prominently in any new scare about chemical or biological attack. In fact, it is one of the less likely forms of warfare to be waged; as we shall see, the real threat from these weapons may come from their use in much more limited wars with more limited objectives. But let us examine the situation in more detail, for undoubtedly the toxic weapons may become capable of really large-scale use.

At the moment there are rather severe limitations on

this form of warfare. The most highly developed weapons in the toxic armory, as we have seen, are the chemical weapons and, of these, the nerve gases are by far the most toxic. One B-52 bomber loaded with nerve gas is said to be capable of producing 30 percent fatalities in an area of 100 square miles. If, purely for convenience, we take an intercontinental war to be concerned with land masses measuring about 2,000 miles square, we are dealing with areas of four million square miles. Clearly it would be impossible to blanket the whole area with nerve gas to produce 30 percent casualties for this would involve at least 40,000 B-52 flights and in the neighborhood of one million tons of nerve gas. However hard the plant in Indiana may be working, the United States can have nothing approaching this amount of nerve gas.

The figures I have quoted are for the nerve gas GB and are theoretical calculations. In practice, nerve gas could not be used with anything like the efficiency assumed in the calculation. Against this must be set the fact that it would never be necessary to blanket an entire continent; at most all that would be required would be to saturate centers of high population density. These two factors tend to cancel one another out. Whatever assumptions are made about the attack, the same answer always comes out: continental scale war with nerve gas would require far larger amounts of nerve gas than are either available or practical. The conclusion is obvious. Continental warfare with nerve gases looks technically very unlikely but the situation could change if compounds much more toxic than even the nerve gases were to be discovered, developed, and stockpiled.

In a sense, such compounds are already known—in the form of microorganisms. Biological weapons, as we have seen, are much more toxic than chemicals. Theoretical calculations show that as little as 100 milliliters of a bacteria-containing suspension might be sufficient to infect everyone breathing the atmosphere in an area of one square kilometer for five minutes. Because this is a theoretical calculation, let us assume the same effect might be achieved in practice by using one liter of suspension. This would weigh about two pounds. To infect an area of one square mile would then require a few pounds of infective material—very different from the amount required to infect the same area with nerve gas. (Using the same theoretical assumptions, one would need several hundred pounds of the nerve gas GB to kill 30 percent of a population breathing the atmosphere for five minutes in an area of one square mile.) By using biological weapons, one could gain by a factor of several hundred in the weight of material that had to be delivered. But the real difference would be that the form of dissemination would be totally different. Rather than sending scores of missiles or bombers to many different sites, one would try to blanket the area with a few large releases of biological material upwind of the land mass to be attacked. One would hope the wind was strong enough to carry the infective material over the entire land mass before it was inactivated by, for instance, ultraviolet radiation from the sun. This presupposes two things: that the wind blows in the right direction at the right strength for the right amount of time; and that bacterial or viral strains have already been developed that will withstand exposure to the atmosphere for the required period and yet still be active enough to carry out their task. I have already dwelt at some length on both these problems. All that need be said here is that it is difficult to believe that we have either the right biological weapons for such an attack or that a military commander would be happy with what is obviously a very chancy method of offense.

So toxic warfare on a continental scale looks currently beyond our capabilities. But it will not necessarily remain so. The discovery of much more toxic chemicals or—and this is perhaps the more likely—the perfection of biological weapons could change the position radically. With the current rate of expenditure on both types of weapon, it is difficult to believe that the necessary technological advances will not be made in the future. What would be the implications of toxic weapons that could be operated reliably on a continental scale?

The first implication, of course, is that a new weapon system will come into existence with the killing power of nuclear weapons but without two of the nuclear disadvantages—high cost and severe ensuing damage to property. One can envisage then talk not only of the nuclear club—meaning those countries in possession of the nuclear weapon—but also talk of the toxic club. The difference would be that the toxic club would number considerably more than the nuclear one. The cheapness of the armory, and its relative technical simplicity compared to nuclear engineering would bring it potentially within range of most nations. And to restrain members of this toxic club from using their weapons would be a good deal more difficult than it has proved to prevent members of the nuclear club from using theirs. The real reason for this would be that there is no such thing as nuclear escalation. There are no incapacitating nuclear weapons and there are no nuclear weapons that simply make the enemy's eyes run. But the temptation to use tear gases in war will always be high, will probably be succumbed to, and could very easily lead to the use of more and more dangerous toxic weapons, culminating in the continental toxic weapons. It is a clean step from conventional warfare to nuclear warfare. The pathway from conventional warfare to toxic warfare on a continental scale is a dirty and slippery slope, down which it would be all too easy to slide.

The existence of a toxic club would have other implications. Some of them might be beneficial. For instance, it would take some of the pressure off middle-sized nations to develop their own nuclear weapons. But I think these are minor considerations compared with the very real threat to world peace that a toxic club would constitute.

I have already mentioned the kind of limited war into which the military struggles between the major powers have now been channeled. Two examples are the wars in Korea and in Vietnam. These have resulted at least partially from the nuclear deadlock and it seems likely that other wars of a similar nature will follow. Both have involved guerrilla warfare, which is also going on in other parts of the world, such as South America. These wars are characterized by what is really a form of ritualized struggle between the world's two major ideologies. They are fought in neutral territory, on the pretext that the political future of that territory is in jeopardy. Essentially the struggle is often between a sophisticated force and a local force operating from concealed and unknown positions in rugged country. Such war rarely becomes an open war until such time as one side decides that its aim must be to win and not just to suppress.

Such operations are difficult to combat with the conventional weapons. The local forces who know the terrain have all the advantages on their side. They ambush and boobytrap against an enemy who cannot retaliate in the same way because he cannot find the guerrilla bases until they have been vacated. If he does find them, they are usually inaccessible to a modern army either from land or from the air. In such a struggle chemical weapons are of great use and biological ones might also be if they were further developed. This implies that if this type of limited war is the likely pattern over the next several years, pressures are going to mount for using more and more sophisticated weapons and possibly even biological ones. These pressures have already been succumbed to in Vietnam and there is every chance chemical escalation will begin there in earnest in the next few years. The Vietnamese situation has been partly responsible for the increased interest of the American authorities in toxic weapons and several of the contracts the Department of Defense has placed with universities have been of direct relevance to the Vietnam war.

One need, of course, is to deprive the guerrilla of his protective forest camouflage. Defoliation has been practiced on a large scale in Vietnam and efforts are being made to find even more effective herbicides with which to spray the jungle. Another related method of getting at guerrilla hideouts is to deprive the local region of its food supply—which is of course normally collected from purely civilian farms or paddy fields. Crop spraying has also been used in Vietnam. Another problem is to drive guerrillas out of underground complexes when these have been discovered. In Vietnam tear gas has been used for this purpose but this has not proved greatly effective. Officials have pressed for permission to use more harmful and persistent compounds, such as mustard gas, but this second step in chemical escalation has so far been denied them.

These are three uses of toxic weapons which have already been used in an antiguerrilla action. One can think of many other possible uses. For instance, because jungle hideouts are so difficult to find, one solution would be to blanket a suspected area with a biological aerosol (if one were available). Admittedly, it would have a severe effect on any civilians who chanced to be in the area and they would probably have to be written off as inevitable casualties. An alternative technique would be to spray one of the V agents (nerve gases) along the known trails of the enemy guerrillas. These agents are so persistent that they would linger for weeks and rub off on the clothing or skin of the guerrillas when they used the trail. Death would follow quickly and suddenly, and this might even start a major panic among the guerrilla force as the cause of death would probably be unknown to them. Biological weapons might also offer a means of preventing subversive infiltration. If all the occupants of South Vietnam were vaccinated against a particular disease, and that disease were then spread as an aerosol, indigenous occupants would be protected but infiltrators would succumb.

When one considers a situation like this, one begins to see how useless a modern army, with its conventional weapons, is against a guerrilla force. When the British were fighting against communist guerrilla forces in Malaya, it took 20 times as many troops as there were guerrillas just to halt their activities. The "cost-effectiveness" of the Vietcong guerrilla technique in Vietnam is estimated to be thousands of times greater than that of the sophisticated American armaments. It even takes an average of 50,000 American bullets to kill one Vietcong guerrilla. The reason is simple enough: most of our modern armaments have evolved via the two world wars—open wars fought on a large scale between two sides, which were roughly balanced against one another. What is going on in Vietnam, and likely to take place in other countries in the future, is a totally different form of struggle in which it would indeed be surprising if "World War" armories found much use. Thus one can see that those who claim that the Americans are using Vietnam as a proving ground for new weapon systems—not just chemicals—probably do so justifiably. The American forces are learning to adapt their methods of waging war to the sort of war that may well typify world struggles for some years to come. For this they will need new weapons and the chemical and biological armory looks among the more promising of these. In other words, we may have reached a turning point in the evolution of military technology. And it would be ironic indeed if the nuclear deadlock, by bringing into existence the limited war, also brought into existence the toxic deadlock.

There is one further aspect of this form of warfare which merits examination. We have seen that two of the problems with biological agents are that they are intrinsically unreliable and that they cannot be effectively tested prior to use in the way that any other weapon would be tested. These factors are clearly major disadvantages if biological weapons were required as a reliable link in a chain of military operations in an open war. But it is possible that they might not be important in a limited war. In fact an operation of the kind going on in Vietnam might be the ideal time for a power to test its biological armory against a guerrilla force. There would be little to lose— assuming the power was prepared to discount the pressures of world opinion. And there might be much to gain. If the weapon proved successful, it might even be decisive in throwing the guerrilla force into confusion. If it failed, it might provide valuable information—as no other field test could—about how to improve the biological armory. I should add that there is so far no reliable information at all that either side in Vietnam has tested any biological weapons in this way. But it would be surprising if the idea had not occurred to those responsible for developing such weapons.

The other main potential form of conflict in which chemical and biological weapons might find a use is sabotage. Here the advantages of lightness are supreme. Whereas it is difficult to kill a single official with conventional weapons simply because of the bulkiness of even small arms, the amount of chemical needed to achieve the same effect would be minute. Similarly, political centers—such as the White House or the Houses of Parliament—would be more easily decimated of their staff with chemical or biological weapons than with any other kind. Such operations could be carried out by secret agents without any great difficulty. Their value in war is more doubtful. There are always replacements for military and political leaders and the main effect of their assassination is often thought to be a stirring up of public alarm and outrage. In recent wars sabotage acts against prominent individuals have not been greatly used. The reason is probably not that they would have been particularly difficult to perform but simply that their value in a large-scale conflict is doubtful. Indeed, they could prove to have a negative value for there is no surer way of producing national cohesion than to kill a well-loved leader—particularly, one would imagine, if it were accomplished with chemical or biological weapons. So the fact that it may soon be much easier to use this form of sabotage against individuals may not count for very much.

But sabotage can be used in other ways. Whereas a minister or a general can be replaced almost overnight, a missile crew, a hospital staff, a government department, or sometimes even an infantry battalion cannot. Small units of men in their own country have not so far constituted an important military target in past wars, mainly because they represent such a difficult objective. To kill 1,000 men in enemy territory requires a huge organization if conventional weapons are to be used. And this kind of action would be almost bound to result in the capture of the attacking personnel. But chemical sabotage presents quite a different picture. A few pounds of nerve gas is all that would be required. With an odorless, colorless gas it would not be very difficult to introduce the chemical into, say, a crowded conference room via the ventilator system or even by an aerosol pack hidden beneath the floorboards. The effect would be catastrophic and could put an important and irreplaceable unit out of action within minutes.

This form of sabotage could be used either to raise public alarm or to put important military groups out of action. The latter, of course, would be considerably more difficult to attack than a civilian group for, if another war ever comes in which this situation becomes likely, such military groups will have to be stringently protected. We have never lived through a war of this kind in the post nerve gas era and there would be many differences from the last war. One would be an elaborate series of chemical detection systems—of the kind I shall discuss in the next chapter—which would have to be continuously monitored. Key military installations would have to be guarded against chemical and biological attack most closely of all.

Sabotage against small groups is likely to involve at most only chemical weapons. There would be little advantage to be gained from using biological weapons and much to be lost—in unreliability and in a much greater time lag, for instance. There is a third form of sabotage, however, in which biological weapons might be used and where their unreliability and unproven value would not represent a necessarily very great handicap. This would be in large-scale attacks on the population, carried out from within enemy territory. Indeed, this is a similar situation to the one we were discussing just now—guerrilla warfare. In both cases, one territory is occupied by both sides—at different locations, of course—and special methods are needed to get at the enemy. The application most often talked about in this context is an attack either on or via food supplies. A few agents might be able to create considerable havoc by the clever introduction of a new crop pest, for instance, which over the course of a year or more could have an alarming though perhaps not decisive effect on the progress of a war. Similarly if agents could gain access to the food-processing industries they might well be able to introduce chemicals or biological material into foods which are not normally cooked in the home before being eaten—bread, milk, corned beef, and similar products would be obvious objectives. But here there would be a real advantage in using biological agents for most have an incubation period of at least a week. By the time the cause of the food poisoning had been tracked down, tens of thousands might have eaten the contaminated food. With chemicals the warning would come much more quickly and there would be that much more time for evasive action.

In future wars, these are real threats. In some ways they may sound more alarming than perhaps they would turn out to be in practice. I have just said that a post nerve gas war will be markedly different from any previous war. One of the differences that would be noticed most would be the elaborate defense systems against chemical and biological attack that will be used. Though these are difficult to devise—as we shall see in the next chapter—they probably would protect quite well against sabotage.

CHAPTER 9

Prevention Is Better than Cure

Any method which appears to offer advantages to a nation at war will be vigorously employed by that nation. There is but one logical course to pursue, namely, to study the possibilities of such warfare from every angle, make every preparation for reducing its effectiveness, and thereby reduce the likelihood of its use.

G. W. Merck
(in report on biological warfare
to the U.S. Secretary of War, 1942)

IN THE VERY EARLY DAYS of chemical warfare, defense was simple. It involved two cheap and readily available commodities: hot, soapy water and supportive treatment. The idea was that the victim should be thoroughly washed to remove any trace of liquid chemicals with which he might be contaminated, and that he should be put to bed. His temperature would be taken every few hours, he would be made as comfortable as is possible in the face of, say, mustard blisters, and the nursing staff would hope he would not die. There was little else that could be done. Today a great deal more can be done. Defense authorities in both the United States and the United Kingdom have revealed a little about their countries' preparations for defense against toxic warfare and a good deal of information has been produced by other sources. But the available evi-

172

dence does suggest that civilian defense preparations are not very elaborate and might not be very effective in protecting the civilians who are likely to be the principal target of any large chemical or biological attack. Only in neutral Sweden, for example, is it known that there is an effective gas mask available for every man, woman, and child living in that country.

I do not want to give the impression that either the United States or the United Kingdom is neglecting the field of defense. Even in Britain there are two establishments at Porton whose tasks are officially concerned only with defense against these weapons. Establishments such as these, and their equivalents in the United States, have produced many effective prototypes of gas masks, protective suits, detection and warning systems, mass inoculation vaccination guns, and so on, which represent considerable advances over anything previously available. But a prototype instrument or piece of equipment is not much good in the face of a chemical or biological attack. It has to be developed into a production model and then produced in quantity. At the present time, neither the United States nor the United Kingdom will admit to holding sufficient stockpiles of gas masks to protect all their civilians. No news is said to be good news. In this case it means either that officials attach a very low probability to a large-scale chemical or biological attack against civilians—which is good news—or that they see little point in trying to protect the civilian population if one does occur—which is, by any account and in spite of the proverb, bad news.

But defense against chemical and biological attack involves more than gas masks. What is required is a complete defense system, such as exists against enemy aircraft attack or some of the other more conventional weapons. The latter at least have the advantage that it is easy to tell when they are being used. The same would not necessarily be true of chemical or biological weapons. Of course, tear gas, mustard gas, and similar agents are quickly felt by their smell and have an almost immediate physiological effect. But some of the nerve gases and all the biological weapons are odorless and colorless and their effects may take from several minutes to several weeks to appear. Furthermore, they are capable of producing their effect during the time in which they go undetected. Nerve gas, for instance, may not be detected for several minutes by which time an incapacitating if not a lethal dose could have been inhaled. A few organisms of Q-fever could be inhaled during an attack and start an infection that would not become apparent to the victim for several days. If pneumonic plague is not treated within 24 hours of exposure, it produces virtually a 100 percent mortality.

The four minute warning of a nuclear attack seems long in comparison with what is ideally required of a system to give warning of a chemical or biological attack. In four minutes untold damage might be done to a population, particularly by nerve gas. What is required is a system that gives an instantaneous warning—in the form of a siren, for instance—as soon as the first traces of chemicals or microorganisms become apparent. It is difficult to develop such apparatus if only because it must be capable of distinguishing chemicals from all the other dirt and smoke particles that are characteristic of air over a battlefield. Such a system must be fully automatic and constantly in use. Several types are being made available to the armed forces, although they all have a number of disadvantages. Most of them sample air at only one specific location and so run the severe risk that while they are recording no chemical contamination, and emitting no warning signal, another location only a few hundred yards away may be saturated with a highly toxic concentration of gas. Clearly such a localized detector must be placed upwind of the forces it is designed to give warning to, and this means that it must be light and portable so that it can be placed in a different position whenever the wind changes. A warning system of this kind does not necessarily need to identify the type of chemical being used in attack. As soon as its siren is heard, the procedure will be the same regardless of whether mustard gas, nerve gas, or a bacterial aerosol is being used. All personnel will immediately hold their breath and put on their standard gas mask, which is designed to give protection against any chemical or biological agent.

What is really needed here is a different system altogether—one which gives warning, and takes air samples, over a much wider area. A type of chemical radar is being developed by the Americans and is known as LOPAIR (standing for long path infrared). The idea is that the chemicals likely to be used in attack will absorb infrared radiation. An infrared beam is thus directed at a mirror about a quarter of a mile away which reflects the beam to a special detector. This determines whether or not infrared radiation of specific wavelengths has been absorbed to an unusual extent during the beam's passage to the mirror and back. If it has, the detector can, in theory, identify the chemical responsible and estimate roughly its concentration. Equipment of this kind could be much more effective than small local detectors. If the mirror could be eliminated and reflections picked up from distant trees or mountains, as Rothschild has suggested, the beam could be swept round in a circle, just like a radar, and could cover a huge area. But the technical difficulties would be immense. For one thing, infrared radiation is strongly absorbed in any case by an atmosphere containing an appreciable amount of water vapor. This means that the detection of the returning signal requires sensitive equipment. If the mirror were eliminated, it would have to be more sensitive by several orders of magnitude.

So far these problems have not been satisfactorily solved and LOPAIR is still under development. But the kind of technique involved was given a technological boost by the discovery of the laser—a source of very brilliant light or infrared radiation—in the early 1960s. The laser can emit such a powerful beam that there is much more chance of picking up the returning radiation even without a mirror. Experiments have been carried out at Edgewood Arsenal, for instance, to see if a laser system could be used to detect chemical aerosols. So far the instrument has proved rather successful at measuring the relative numbers of particles of different sizes in the atmosphere and this, as we shall see, might have implications for a biological detection system. But the laser beam also suffers from the disadvantages of atmospheric absorption and it is too soon to tell whether it will provide an effective warning or detection system.

This problem of advance warning is so difficult that a different defense philosophy is beginning to emerge. In the event of combat likely to involve chemical and biological weapons, personnel will be trained to don protective clothes—respirators and gloves, at a minimum—on the first indication of any delivery of toxic weapons. This might take the form of a low flying aircraft or the arrival of shells, particularly those producing a reduced explosive impact.

The problem then is to know when to remove protective equipment. To this end a residual vapor detector is being made available to British forces at the section level—one would be issued to the leader of every ten men. It is replacing an earlier and now obsolete model and will give troops a clear indication of when the air is sufficiently uncontaminated to breathe without protection. Although effective for use in a chemical attack, it has no use in the event of a biological one.

The problems involved in identifying the chemicals used in an attack present no great technical difficulty. Chemical kits are available for testing for chemicals; these also identify the particular ones being used and give an estimate of their concentration. Some are based on quite simple color reactions with other chemicals and provide, in effect, a litmus paper for chemical warfare. Some are literally based on impregnated paper, others on tubes of chemicals through which a sample of the suspected air is passed. British troops likely to be involved in this kind of war will be issued a small patch of material sewn on to their battle dress. If liquid chemical comes into contact with it, the patch will change color immediately and give the soldier an indication of the chemical attack. If he finds that liquid chemical has landed on him, he will use special pads which are part of his standard equipment to wipe it off. So, once it is known that a chemical attack is in progress standard equipment, which can be used by almost any soldier with a minimum of training, is available to identify the chemical and estimate its concentration. Once this is done, the word would be passed by radio up the line that the attack was in progress and that it involved, say, nerve gas or mustard gas.

But the problems involved in warning, detection, and identification of biological attack are even more difficult to solve. This is all the more serious because of the long delay between attack and illness characteristic of biological attack. Whereas one battalion or town attacked by nerve gas, even if it had no detection equipment, would begin to feel the effects inside a few minutes and could therefore warn the next town or battalion by radio before the wind had had time to transport the chemical there, no such procedure could be used in biological warfare.

There are two possible ways in which a warning system might be devised. The first is that we know a biological attack is likely to be made with aerosols with particle diameters of between about 1 and 5 microns. Any attack of this kind is therefore likely to be accompanied by an unnaturally large rise in the proportion of particles in the atmosphere of this size range. So a warning system could be based, in theory, on this fact alone. It would not involve any kind of analysis of the nature of the particles; the very fact that they were of this particular size would be sufficient to indicate that a biological attack was probably being made.

Several attempts have been made, in the United States, Britain, Sweden, and elsewhere, to develop a system which measures particle size in this way. They can be automated and, up to a point, they can also be made to work. Their main disadvantage is that they are essentially local devices, which sample the air in only one given place. They are also rather liable to give a false alarm if given an overdose of cigarette smoke or car exhaust. All such devices are still in the experimental stage. It is easy enough to see why. They would have to detect the equivalent of one infectious particle in a liter of air which also contained up to 100 similar but mainly noninfectious and naturally occurring particles. Some of these natural particles are bound to fall in the same size range as a biological aerosol. The implication is that a device of this kind must sample huge quantities of air if it has any chance of being reliable.

The second means of providing some form of alarm

against biological attack is to try and identify some particular chemical characteristic of microorganisms. All such living forms contain protein and it is possible to use experimental techniques that will monitor the protein content of an air sample. But the main difficulty again is that there is always a background protein content in the atmosphere—in the form of naturally occurring microorganisms and other material—which is difficult to distinguish from microorganisms being used in a biological attack. Such protein counters would also be essentially local devices and every time one was set up it would have to be calibrated with the average background protein count of that particular area for that particular season and for the particular weather conditions which were prevailing.

The same limitations apply to another device being developed at the Goddard Space Flight Center for nonmilitary purposes. This Goddard detector is known as Firefly because it depends on chemicals extracted from the tail of the firefly that glow when exposed to adenosine triphosphate (ATP), another chemical found in most living organisms and which does not occur naturally. The firefly tail contains reduced luciferin and an enzyme known as luciferase, together with magnesium ions. If ATP is present, the reduced luciferin is oxidized, the ATP is reduced, and light is emitted. This is how fireflies glow. The Firefly device actually makes use of the enzyme luciferase, which cannot be synthesized. It weighs only about a pound and might eventually be used to detect as little as 10^{-17} grams of ATP —about the amount contained in a single organic cell. Although this device was developed as a possible means for detecting unusual life forms in outer reaches of the earth's atmosphere—and possibly on other planets—it might find a use as a biological warfare detection system. It would have a somewhat limited use, however, for it would not be able to detect virus agents, which contain no ATP.

The field of study in which scientists borrow ideas from nature and adapt them for their own use—as in Firefly—is one which may hold considerable promise for biological detection systems as well as for chemical ones. For instance, the Army Research Office in the United States has funded a contract with the Aeronutronic Division of Philco Corporation to develop a "man-made" nose capable of detecting minute traces of strange chemicals. Some scientists believe that the systems used by many forms of life to detect chemicals have something in common and, if this could be understood, it might provide great advances in our ability to detect minute concentrations of both chemical and biological materials. If such a "biosensor" were ever developed it would find many applications in fields other than biological and chemical warfare. The Philco scientists are studying the olfactory system of the greenfly and have tried to make an artificial model of it. I should stress that both the Goddard and the Philco work are "way-out"; they are not at the moment developing into effective military equipment.

From what has been said, it is clear that warning, detection, and identification systems for chemical agents are more advanced, even if only for military use, than those for biological agents. In some countries civil defense workers are also familiar with the simpler types of apparatus and preparations in this field are also quite well advanced. The same is not true of the equivalent biological systems which for the most part are still in the laboratory stage or nearing the point at which they require field testing (always a delicate operation, and a politically sensitive one, with biological weapons). Probably some forms of detection system could be got on to a production basis if the likelihood of biological warfare increases within the fairly near future. But there is a need for a greater research effort in this field and it is one to which Pugwash— as we shall see in Chapter 10—is devoting some attention.

Efforts have also been made to set up a scale of risk of biological, and to a lesser extent, chemical warfare. Biological attacks will depend critically on atmospheric conditions and the prevailing weather. So clearly there will be days on which attacks of this kind could be deemed very unlikely and days on which they would seem much more feasible. A scale could be set up, like those used in regions liable to forest fires, indicating the likelihood of attack. Such techniques have helped in forest fire areas and they might well do so in chemical or biological warfare— but they would not, of course, make detection systems any less essential.

Although it is relatively easy to identify the chemical that might be used in a chemical attack, it is not at all easy to identify those used in a biological attack. There is no known way of identifying microorganisms with simple color reactions with other chemicals, mainly because the organisms themselves contain such a great variety of chemicals. Identification of microorganisms by characteristic chemicals is not yet feasible and may never be—although as we shall see one bacterial technique does show promise.

The problem is made that much more serious because there is no certainty that the disease used can be identified quickly even when it begins to exert a physiological effect. Many of the diseases likely to be used in biological warfare have very similar initial symptoms such as headache, nausea, fever, and dizziness. Furthermore, if a mixture of diseases was being used in the attack, the pathological picture might well become impossibly complicated.

Specific identification is ultimately essential because the type of drugs and their dosages needed to treat the disease vary considerably with each disease. There is no blanket cure for biological warfare diseases, and in a few cases advance treatment with the wrong drug can be harmful. However, a question of priorities is involved. Treatment with broad action antibiotics is much more likely to be useful than not and current philosophy is that British servicemen would be issued with a broad spectrum antibiotic pack if biological warfare seemed likely.

The standard medical practices for identifying diseases often take 24-48 hours and sometimes a great deal longer. The first requirement is to grow the organisms in culture— and again the type of culture in which they will grow depends a good deal on the type of organism involved. This means that a wide range of culture media and tissues must be kept constantly on the ready. Once a culture has been started, attempts will be made to identify the strain using the microscope, specific antigens and the effect of the culture on other animals, such as guinea pigs, after injection. All these techniques take time. They all require the services of extremely experienced diagnosticians and none is anything like automated. Often a culture cannot be started simply by taking an air sample in which the biological aerosol is thought to be contained. This means that the microorganism must be extracted from the patient and this always involves taking in extra living material for analysis, which may well throw the diagnostician off the track.

One of the newer and more promising techniques for speeding up the process is known as the fluorescent antibody technique. This depends on the ability of certain chemicals that react with the microorganisms to fluoresce when exposed to ultraviolet light. In this way Venezuelan equine encephalitis virus, for instance, has been identified within four hours of being collected from the blood of an infected patient; a very dilute aerosol of the tularemia organism has even been identified within two minutes. But the technique is a new one and it requires special apparatus and specially trained personnel. Although it can be used with bacteria, viruses, and fungi, it is not yet applicable to all members of all groups and it is not clear how the selection of new strains of the type that would be used in biological warfare would affect the process. This is because to make the sample fluoresce it must first be labeled with an antiserum to which a fluorescent dye has been attached. The antiserum will combine with material from only a specific type of bacterium or virus; if it does combine, it will fluoresce under the microscope but if the organism is of a different type there will be no fluorescence. In other words, the technique depends on first having available a range of antisera specific to the microorganisms which are being tested for. If a new and previously unknown form is used, there is a possibility that none of the standard agents will produce the fluorescent effect.

In 1967 another technique was reported, which could eventually speed the identification of microorganisms very considerably. The culture is first centrifuged and the volatile products separated and passed through an apparatus known as a gas chromatograph—a standard piece of laboratory equipment that can identify and quantify individual chemicals. Scientists have found that the volatile products of metabolism which bacteria produce appear to represent a kind of bacterial "fingerprint"—they appear to be limited to about 13 in number and their relative proportions are specific for the type of bacteria. Specific patterns for a number of different strains have already been identified and the technique appears to be ex-

tremely sensitive. During biological warfare it could aid
greatly in identifying the disease being used with speed.
Some bacteria have been identified with this technique in
as little as 30 minutes.

Though the standard methods of identifying bacteria
and viruses are reliable they are all fairly time consuming.
Newer methods promise to speed up the process to such
an extent that most organisms could be identified within
a matter of a few hours. There is, however, no guarantee
that the particular types or strains used in a biological
attack would be common ones and they might take longer
to identify than normally. This is particularly serious because it is possible that the first indication of a biological
attack may be the outbreak of disease symptoms: as I have
explained, the early warning systems, which ought to be
able to detect the attack while it is being made, are poorly
developed and may be difficult to perfect. Furthermore,
the rush to identify the disease when it begins to affect the
attacked population or troops physically will be of vital
importance. Only after the disease has been identified can
correct treatment be prescribed. Wrong treatment of an in-
correctly identified disease could make matters worse. But
before dealing in more detail with treatment, we should discuss the types of protection available, which might make
treatment unnecessary.

The most obvious is the gas mask. This has been rede-
signed almost countless times since the First World War
and is now a good deal improved. Most armies in the world
have stockpiles of gas masks of varying efficiency but
few countries—Sweden is the most notable exception—
have anything like enough to protect their civilians. The
Americans have developed three special masks—one for
military personnel, a similar one for civil defense workers
and a third, less sturdy one for the civilian population.

All are claimed to be almost 100 percent leakproof to chemical and biological weapons as well as to radioactive fallout. The civilian mask is available in six sizes because fit between the mask and the contour of the face is crucial —remember that as few as perhaps 10 organisms of some diseases might be sufficient to cause infection. If a gas mask is to be of any use at all in such conditions, it has to be as near 100 percent perfect as makes no difference. Most of them are.

The new British respirator is known as the S.6. It has been designed to allow easier breathing, wide range of vision (but still somewhat limited), and greater comfort. It is manufactured commercially, is available for export, and is issued as personal equipment to every serviceman in BAOR and other arenas where the occasion warrants it. This, of course, is an "action respirator" and is more sophisticated than the type that would be required for civilian protection. Several million older but post-World War II respirators are stockpiled in Britain for civilian defense and batches of them are periodically tested to ensure their operational viability.

Respirators are designed to fulfill two different purposes. The first is to absorb any chemicals with which the air may be contaminated before they can be inhaled. As the range of chemicals which might be used is so vast, the absorption device on a modern mask is designed not to react chemically with known compounds but to absorb physically any contaminants present. This means that the modern mask is proof not only against the latest nerve gases but should be useful even if further and as yet unidentified chemicals are developed as weapons. The other function of masks is to filter out—but not absorb— aerosol particles of the kind that might be dispersed in a biological attack. They are designed to filter particles between 1 and 5 microns in diameter, the typical size range likely to be used, more effectively than other sizes.

In spite of the funds which have been spent on chemical and biological weapons in the past few years, it appears that not even the Americans have provided sufficient masks for civilians. At various times over the past decade, civil defense workers in the United States have lobbied for more funds to be devoted to putting a mask into production in such quantity that everyone could be protected. So far this has not been done, although plans have been drawn up for a mask, which would sell at about $2-4; an infant protector, for children too young to wear masks, has also been designed. But clearly progress in the civilian field has not been as rapid as was at one time expected. In 1960 the Office of Civil Defense estimated that they needed 700,000 masks for civil defense workers; at that time they had only 85,000. Plans were made to close the gap by 1967 but they were not carried out. It seems strange that a country which has spent so much on the development and stockpiling of toxic weapons—and therefore presumably sees an urgent need for them—should not see an equally urgent need to protect its civilians who are, after all, as likely to suffer from a biological if not a chemical attack as are military personnel. Yet when more funds are needed for chemical and biological weapons, U.S. officials are quick to point out that this situation arises because of the preparations their potential enemies are making in the same field. If this is true, surely a greater proportion of their funds should be devoted to civilian protection.

The respirator, of course, protects only the individual. There is a good deal to be said for various plans which have been suggested to provide fallout shelters—proof against both chemical and biological weapons—in place of masks. Of course, shelters alone would be of little use to troops who must remain active but they could perhaps provide sufficient protection for civilians. The major problem would arise during the time lapse between warning of a toxic attack and actually arriving in the shelter. But if the shelters were family ones—or perhaps shared by groups of three or four families—this time lapse would amount to only a few minutes. By taking a minimum of breaths, and by covering the mouth and nose with a folded handkerchief—which acts as quite an efficient temporary filter—most of the danger might be eliminated. Estimates made in the early 1960s suggested that the cost of a do-it-yourself shelter for fallout protection was then between $150 and $200 per family. Making it proof against chemical and biological weapons would perhaps double its cost and defense workers in general concluded that it would be cheaper to provide masks. Since then, the cost of pumps and filters has come down and various types of fiber board have become available, which might filter off most biological organisms yet allow the exhaled carbon dioxide and water vapor to pass through. But any decision to equip a civilian population with shelters of this kind cannot be taken in isolation or after consideration of the risks of only toxic attack. There was a time when the need for shelters against radioactive fallout was thought urgent. In the United States it was estimated that the total cost would be about $6,000 million spread over five years. If the decision is ever taken to provide shelters for all civilians against nuclear attack, it would clearly be wise to take the extra precaution of making the shelters proof against chemical and biological weapons as well. There would, of course, be an extra cost but it would certainly be cheaper than also providing a second, antitoxic shelter. And it would seem to be a more logical step than providing civilians with both antifallout shelters and with gas masks.

Service personnel, of course, would be provided with both masks and with shelters for some special operations in which it is inconvenient to wear masks. The U.S. Army has designed a number of different Army shelters and of course has investigated the range of problems that arises in trying to protect Army personnel while they are carrying out the diverse range of jobs characteristic of a modern army. Both British and American soldiers would also be issued protective clothing in the event of a toxic attack. This clothing would consist of a suit, a hood, special boots, and gloves. What is known as a CB suit was specially developed at Porton in the 1960s. Technically it is a notable advance in that it is extremely light and virtually leakproof. It is now being made available to British servicemen in special areas. It presumably has similarities with American patterns for both governments cooperate fairly closely on many defense aspects including some of those concerned with chemical and biological warfare.

If chemical or biological war ever breaks out, we shall have to rely heavily on detection and identification systems, gas masks, protective clothing, and filtered shelters. The only other line of defense—to protect troops or civilians from attack in advance or to cure them afterwards— is fraught with practical difficulty. There are many reasons for this. One is that there are still some biological agents against which it is impossible to provide any form of advance medical protection. Another is that even with the diseases that can be cured the administrative difficulties involved in treating disease on this scale have never been encountered in peacetime and look formidably difficult in practice. A third is that by the time a major proportion of a population has been put out of action to the extent that it requires hospitalization or systematic treatment, the enemy may already have achieved his purpose. Against this must be put the fact that the medical aspects of defense are not wholly or even primarily the concern of defense departments. On the contrary, the treatment of disease with antibiotics and the development of new and improved vaccines form the mainstay of civilian medical research. And for those diseases which occur naturally with some frequency, medical research has already provided much information of defense value. Unhappily, many of the diseases that might be used in biological warfare are not at all common and receive scant attention from civilian research.

During the two world wars much effort was devoted to improving the treatment of the effects of standard chemical agents such as mustard gas and phosgene. Ointments have been developed to treat the blister agents, antidotes are available for use against blood gases and many other chemicals have been investigated to see if they could be used to provide protection in advance against any form of chemical attack. The result of all this work is that it is now possible to speed the recovery of patients who fall victim to almost any of the standard, conventional chemicals. But the blisters produced by mustard gas are extremely disabling and, once formed, will take weeks to disappear completely, even with the best medical treatment in the world. Certainly treatment can minimize the suffering involved but this does not materially affect the outcome of a chemical attack. By the time victims have been cured forces would have been put out of action and the local objective of the attack would have been accomplished. The fact that chemical agents produce casualties who can be medically treated does not alter their military value in any substantial way. There is only one way round this problem. Physical defense—by means of rapid warning systems and gas masks—would have to be made so effective that these gases never got a chance to exert their intended effect.

The nerve gases pose the most difficult problems. For one thing these are primarily lethal agents and the object of treatment is therefore to save life. Secondly, they act with great speed and this means that any treatment involved must take place within a few minutes of exposure. In other words, it must be on the battlefield, not in the hospital. On the other hand, the nerve gases act through a very specific biochemical action on chemicals involved in the transmission of nerve impulses. This means that they are more prone to chemical treatment than, say, the much more generalized and destructive power of mustard gas. In the event, it was shown that a powerful antidote for nerve gas does exist in the form of atropine or belladonna. The name comes from one of its other properties, that of causing dilatation of the eye; legend has it that Spanish beauties used it in this way to increase "eye appeal." Atropine, which has the formula $C_{17}H_{23}O_3N$ and is an alkaloid, has a range of other useful and more medical properties. Among these is the fact that it acts as an antidote for anticholinesterases. Nerve gases, as I have explained in Chapter 3, exert their effect by inactivating the enzyme cholinesterase in its job of breaking acetylcholine into two parts so that the nerve can be fired again. Put simply, atropine prevents the nerve gases from acting as anticholinesterases. But the antidote must be applied very promptly if it is to work. In other words, no soldier or civilian would have time to seek medical advice. This is made more complicated by the fact that no oral form of atropine is yet available; it has to be injected into the bloodstream. For these reasons the British and American forces in theatres where chemical warfare is likely carry a small automatic injection device already loaded with atropine. It is held against the thigh, the button pushed and atropine is injected. It is a simple device and has been proved effective. Automatic injector and atropine supplies are readily available in Britain and the United States which, in 1960, was estimated to have 5 million doses stockpiled. Altogether there are three types available, one developed in the United States, one in the United Kingdom, and one in Sweden. The British model has the unique advantage that if the needle strikes the bone—as is liable to happen—pressure is released and the progress of the needle automatically halted. This prevents complications which can set in if atropine is injected into bone tissue. Three auto-injectors are now standard issue to every British serviceman operating in areas thought remotely likely ever to witness chemical attack and similar equipment was carried by Israeli soldiers during the 1967 war.

Further research is now being devoted to improving the chemical treatment of nerve gas poisoning. Some of this has gone on in conjunction with the manufacturers of those insecticides that have chemical affinities with the nerve gases (which were, of course, originally discovered in a hunt for better insecticides). One product of this research has been the discovery that treatment with atropine is greatly improved if accompanied by treatment with a drug known as an oxime. One type, known as P2S, has been developed in Britain and is already in use against cases of insecticide poisoning. It seems likely that oxime therapy will develop a good deal in the future.

Death from nerve gas poisoning is due to asphyxia because the respiratory muscles become inoperative. It follows that artificial respiration can sometimes be used to save life if atropine is not available or if it is applied too late. But it is a mistake to assume that what we normally know as artificial respiration has any effect at all. Most of the techniques used in cases of drowning or electric shock depend on starting the breathing cycle by completing one half of it—depressing the diaphragm, for instance —and letting the body itself complete the second. This does not work in the case of nerve gas poisoning, for the respiratory muscles are completely inoperative and the whole of the breathing cycle must be reproduced artificially if natural breathing is to be resumed. To this end the Chemical Defence Experimental Establishment at Porton has developed a simple portable bellows resuscitator, which is used to treat coal gas poisoning and drowning and has proved more effective than the "kiss of life."

From what has been said, it seems clear that an attack on civilians with nerve gas might well produce more casualties than any other kind of weapon. It is true, of course, that the dual defense of gas mask and atropine, issued to all civilians, might prove effective. But it would first require intensive training of the civilian population for the gas mask and antidote are effective only if used within minutes after an attack has begun. What the response of civilians to a nerve gas attack would be depends primarily on how much they know about it. Today most civilians are reasonably versed in the jargon of nuclear warfare and they know something of the effects of radiation blast and fallout. But they know next to nothing of nerve gas. In wartime ignorance and fear of the unknown lead frequently to mass panic. A greatly increased public understanding of modern chemical warfare is needed if civilian casualties in such a war are ever to be minimized. And in the long run a better understanding of the problems is likely to lead to better chances of eliminating the threat of chemical warfare altogether.

The medical defenses against biological warfare are totally different. And, in one sense, the situation is more hopeful. There are possibilities of protecting a population in advance against attack and most diseases that are likely to be used can be cured. These weapons also take much longer to produce serious effects than do chemical agents so there is a better chance of organizing serious medical attention for the ill. But because biological weapons might be used to attack very large populations the problem is as much one of quantity as of quality: huge medical resources would be needed, ranging from vast supplies of vaccine and antibiotics to armies of medical orderlies. It follows that there is less to fear from a small-scale biological attack than from a large-scale one. In fact, the number of deaths and casualties are likely to rise disproportionately as the size of the attack increases.

The ideal defense against biological warfare would take the form of a simple pill that would give lasting and full protection against all diseases when taken in advance of an attack, just as a daily dose of paludrin gives protection in advance of the bite from a malarial mosquito. Medical science, of course, has not yet produced such an all pur-pose pill and it will be a long time before it does. Mean-while we shall have to rely first on the other established techniques of disease protection and secondly on estab-lished techniques of curing diseases.

There are very few paludrin-like protectives against the diseases of biological warfare. Instead we would have to rely entirely on vaccines and toxoids. The difficulty here is that, as I have said, the antiviral vaccines are more effec-tive than the antibacterial ones. The vaccines against yel-low fever and smallpox are particularly well developed and there is no doubt that a large population could be given effective protection against both diseases. But one would have to be fairly certain that one or other of these was likely to be used for the expense would be huge.

There are even greater difficulties with the other diseases. Satisfactory vaccines against glanders, melioidosis, psittacosis, and coccidioidomycosis have still not been produced. The vaccines against the other diseases mentioned in Table II are of varying efficiency. Few will protect 100 percent of a population and few will give protection in the face of a really massive dose of the kind that is likely to be administered during biological war. At the moment it is quite inconceivable that a population could be given vaccines against all the possible diseases. Even if it were, the effect would be only short lasting. The plague vaccine, for instance, is still far from satisfactory. Although presumably protected against plague, a scientist at the M.R.E. in Porton died from that disease in 1962. At the time all staff working on plague or likely to come into contact with it received a yearly injection of plague booster. The booster is now given to staff twice yearly. Again, the cost of giving twice-yearly boosters to a large population for even one disease would be enormous.

Scientists working at laboratories concerned with defense against biological warfare have devoted considerable attention to improving both the vaccines and the techniques by which they are delivered. One result of this work has been the injection gun with which up to 700 people can be vaccinated in an hour. Another result is the development of multiple vaccines, which would give protection against at least two or three diseases at the same time. Such vaccines are already used on domestic animals and are now undergoing human trials. The ideal, of course, would be to develop a kind of aerosol vaccine, which required no injection. This would not only be easier to apply but might also be more effective for the aerosol route is the one most likely to be used to produce the infection during war. Many years ago the Russians claimed to have given immunity to volunteers by exposing them to an aerosol of attenuated anthrax, plague, tularemia, and brucellosis germs. This would be the ideal form of protection for both civilians and troops but the Russian work was reported a long time ago and little has been heard of it since. Unhappily, the perfection of this technique still seems a long way off.

Much has been written about the possibilities of curing disease induced by biological attack. I have already indicated that this does not seem likely to influence the decision to make a biological attack or to alter its possible effects. The aim of an attack is to make the enemy ill to such an extent that his resistance to, say, invasion will be substantially altered. Whether or not the plague victim is bed-ridden and dying or bed-ridden and responding to a lengthy treatment with antibiotics will not affect the outcome very much. For this reason I do not intend to deal in detail with the medical treatment of diseases. Suffice to say that there are still some diseases that are virtually incurable. These include many virus diseases but, perhaps more important for our purposes, they also include the bacterial diseases cholera and melioidosis, and botulism. Unhappily, few of the likely diseases can be treated during the period between infection and development of symptoms. If this could be done, the whole question of medical defense against biological attack might take on a different complexion. But at the moment antibiotics administered during this period do little more than delay the onset of disease for a few days. In one or two exceptional cases the result can actually be harmful.

The treatment of diseases produced in biological warfare is therefore more a question of human survival than of military strategy. Of course, this requires that massive stockpiles of antibiotics be held in readiness and that serious consideration be given as to how many field hospitals could be flown in to infected areas in an attempt to minimize the consequences of the attack. But these are really only *ad hoc* solutions to the problem. What is required is a far more basic approach to the problem and one which, incidentally, would have a huge medical payoff. If an all purpose pill could be produced, or treatment discovered that would be effective during the period between infection and outbreak of disease, it is not inconceivable that the whole idea of biological warfare would begin to look as old fashioned as the bow and arrow. And the boost it would give to medical science and human health needs no emphasis.

Such developments are still a long way off but a greater research effort in this area might bring them nearer. At the moment blanket cures for human disease seem to many doctors to be too near the realms of science fiction to be given much serious attention. But they will undoubtedly come; the really important question is whether or not they come before the biological weapons themselves are perfected and before international law against these weapons becomes worth no more than the piece of paper upon which it is written.

CHAPTER 10

The Mathematics of Suffering

Even with so-called non-lethal agents, some deaths will result. These are to be expected in infants, elderly people and those already suffering from serious disease.

Col. Dan Crovier,
Fort Detrick
(*Weapons Technology*, March-April 1965)

A FEW YEARS AGO an American war game was carried out to simulate a military situation in the Far East. A large Chinese army was considered to be advancing from South Vietnam into Cambodia. To halt the march, a simulated biological strike was called for. When Chemical Corps personnel came to analyze the results, they were so alarming that the State Department made a vain attempt to keep them quiet. For, along with the 75 percent of the enemy troops assumed to be killed or incapacitated, there were 600,000 neutral or friendly civilian casualties. The action had been militarily successful but had produced a devastating effect on the local civilian population, killing or wounding as many people as might be put out of action by a small atomic blast.

The reason, of course, is simply that no toxin or microorganism is known that is specific for military personnel. If biological weapons are ever used on a large scale, they are likely to be used specifically as anticivilian weapons. They will be used selectively to attack civilian populations for these are normally grouped in centers of high population density, which make good targets for biological attack. Troops, on the other hand, are often more dispersed and in any future war are also likely to be much better protected against biological attack. Lastly, biological weapons are bound to produce their greatest effect on the weakest members of any population—those in poor health anyway, those who are old or very young, and those who are pregnant. None of these categories, it must be noted, are likely to be involved in active military service.

Any large-scale biological attack is bound to produce huge civilian casualties. This is true of no other weapon. Many weapons *can* produce the same effect but no others *necessarily* do so. Nuclear weapons, for instance, are capable of producing immense numbers of civilian casualties. But their role in war might be different; they might be used to knock out missile bases, for instance. Biological weapons, as we hear so often, do not destroy property—and this, it is argued, is one reason why they are potentially so valuable. But it is also the reason that makes them the only specifically anticivilian weapon in the world; this is the only task for which they are even remotely suited. If past figures of civilian casualties are anything to go by, it is also the reason why biological weapons are being so actively investigated at the present time. In World War I, 5 percent of those killed were civilians; in World War II, 48 percent were civilians; in Korea, 84 percent were civilians and in Vietnam the percentage is probably even higher. If this trend is to be continued, the biological armory offers the best chance of producing wars in which more than 90 percent of those killed will be civilians.

The question of to what extent civilian populations are

likely to be the principal if not the secondary target of biological warfare involves more than moral issues; it also involves international law. There are two kinds of international law in force—the purely formal kind, such as the Geneva Protocol itself, and the informal kind which is known as international customary law. Though the second type might seem to nonspecialists to be of too nebulous a nature to be of much worth, lawyers regard both types as being equally binding. Both types imply that the fundamental distinction between combatants and civilians in war is one of the basic principles of the law of war. Although violated during the world wars, these laws still apply (as do national laws about burglary and murder, which have been violated far more frequently). They are interpreted to mean that in war attacks must not be directed specifically at civilian populations and, further, that attacks carried out against legitimate targets must not cause civilian damage out of proportion to their military advantage. These principles have been laid down in many forms and by many bodies, particularly the Hague Convention Rules of Land Warfare, the U.N. Genocide Convention of 1948 and the International Military Tribunal held in Nuremburg in 1947-48. They represent an utterly binding sanction against the use of biological warfare because it is virtually impossible to see how a biological attack could be implemented without involving civilian populations to a degree out of proportion to its military advantage.

But there are other objections to biological warfare. It is not possible to test such weapons in the way that other weapons are tested. Therefore, there is no guarantee that an epidemic can be prevented, or that its effects will be predictable. For instance, the measles virus is normally regarded as being relatively harmless. But, when introduced in the Fiji Islands in 1875, 20-25 percent of the population died because they were completely unprotected.

It is quite possible that a similar effect might be produced by one of the so-called incapacitating biological agents. While there are no legal restrictions to using weapons that produce unpredictable effects it would still seem morally indefensible to subject any enemy to a new weapon without knowing in advance the most severe effects that might be produced. Furthermore, it seems possible that such an attack could be regarded as experimentation on enemy personnel. If so, it might fall within the same terms of reference as the experiments that featured in the Nuremburg war trials.

There is also the possibility that the introduction of disease on a large scale could affect the balance of nature in other, even more profound ways—as we have seen that it has done when used against crop pests. This is not a point which can be glossed over lightly or passed off as a wooly argument of only theoretical importance. As Martin Kaplan has emphasized in *Bulletin of the Atomic Scientists* (June 1960): "Sudden disbalances in numbers, or the insertion of new infective elements into evolutionally unprepared animal or plant life could, if done to a sufficient degree, produce for an indefinite period an unrecognizable and perhaps unmanageable world from the standpoint of communicable diseases."

There is, in fact, no dividing line between incapacitating and lethal biological weapons. If the weapon is dispersed as an aerosol it would be impossible to achieve a standard dose and the population is anyway not standardly susceptible. An incapacitating disease will certainly kill a proportion of the population, just as the London fog kills a number of Londoners every year.

These arguments show that there are real moral and

legal objections to the use of both lethal and "incapacitating" biological weapons. Arguments against chemical weapons follow on from here, because it is difficult to distinguish in any practical way between chemical and biological weapons. For instance, the usual distinction is that biological warfare involves spreading an agent that is in some way alive—accepting that a virus can be described as living. Yet what is internationally known as one of the most important biological weapons is botulinum toxin—a chemical which is certainly dead and which when used would simply be sprayed as a chemical. It is classified as a biological weapon because it is derived from biological material—the toxin itself can be made only by the bacterium. But, on the other hand, during World War II the British investigated a chemical known as ricin extracted from castor beans. This was known as a chemical weapon. There is clearly no distinct dividing line between chemical and biological agents; one type leads imperceptibly towards the other. If in a war one side used ricin as a chemical weapon, then another could perhaps feel justified in using botulinum toxin; both chemicals are obtained in a similar way. But if the toxin was used, the first side might claim that this was a biological weapon and that it was therefore free to retaliate by using, say, plague or anthrax. Escalation would be all too easy and all too logical. It would also be legal. Ratification of the Geneva Protocol does not preclude the right to retaliate in kind. It can be argued, therefore, that if one side is attacked even with tear gas, the other side could retaliate legally with nerve gas or plague. The legality of this point would hinge on the precise interpretation of "in kind" and whether or not this was a blanket term used to cover all the weapons prohibited by the Geneva Protocol. But it is unlikely that such niceties would be debated for long in the heat of war.

Some people have tried to define biological and chemical weapons in a different way. Biological weapons, they have argued, affect people differentially and tend to select the weakest first; chemicals, by contrast, are standardized in their results and affect all members of a population equally. This might seem a more logical definition, although a less obvious one, but unfortunately it breaks down. Chemicals are already being used to destroy crops in Vietnam and the resulting starvation certainly affects people differentially: the weakest Vietnamese are the first to die from starvation. The result is that the chemical affects the population as would a biological weapon. Further, there is some evidence that even chemical weapons can have a differential effect on a population; "nonlethal" tear gas, for instance, certainly could cause death when used in large quantities against people already suffering from a respiratory complaint. So it seems that chemical and biological weapons do merge into one another and that escalation would bridge the undefinable gap between them easily enough.

This being the case, and there being both moral and legal reasons for not using biological weapons, it follows that chemical weapons should not be used either. Of course, some chemical uses are in many ways preferable to the alternatives—there can be times when it is more humane to use a relatively harmless chemical weapon than conventional arms. But this is only a short-term view; in the long run it might be disastrous, for it is only a small step from tear gas to mustard gas, from mustard gas to nerve gas, from nerve gas to botulinum toxin, and from toxin to plague. Because of the dangers of opening Pandora's box, the only safe course is to use neither chemical nor biological weapons at all during war (tear gas in riot control or civil disturbances might be permitted for there is no danger there of escalation).

Although the escalation argument is perhaps the strongest against the chemical weapons, there are others. Nerve gas, for instance, could produce fatalities on the scale of nuclear weapons. As much time and effort has been devoted to preparing nuclear test ban treaties and to devising international laws to prohibit the use of nuclear weapons, it would seem logical to extend these to include at least the nerve gases, if not other chemical weapons as well. Rather than representing flexible response, an alternative to the choice between conventional and nuclear weapons, the chemicals could also be said to provide a cheap and technically easier means of reaching weapons capable of the destruction of life on the scale of nuclear weapons. Here, admittedly, one is beginning to play tricks with the mathematics of suffering. One is saying, in effect, that we should approve the use of a weapon such as a machine gun, that can kill 100 people in one minute, but not the use of a weapon that can kill 100,000 people in ten minutes. The simple answer is that we should approve neither but, human nature being what it is, the least we can do is to try to prevent the greater of two evils. Furthermore, there is now no prospect of outlawing the machine gun— but there is a prospect of preserving an existing ban on the use of chemicals and we should make haste to do so.

These, then, are the main constraints—moral and legal —against the use of chemical and biological weapons in war. But attempts have also been made to establish toxic weapons as the most humane weapons ever invented. These arguments tend to interpret the word "humane" in a rather limited way, but, for chemical weapons at least, they have some validity in special cases. Obviously the amount of suffering involved in the use of, say, flame-throwers or napalm can be considerably greater than that caused by tear gas (even though the latter may be far from painless). However, any weapon that killed only a small percentage of those enemies it was used on might also claim some distinction as being relatively "humane."

In his book *Tomorrow's Weapons*, General Rothschild quotes figures to support this argument. In World War I the Americans suffered 272,000 casualties; about 70,000 of these—rather more than one quarter—were produced by gas. But only 2 percent of the gas casualties died, compared with 25.8 percent of the other, nongas casualties. In addition, only 4.1 percent of the nonfatal gas casualties were discharged as disabled, compared to 25.4 percent of those who were wounded with other weapons. In other words, proportionately fewer were killed and fewer disabled by chemical weapons. When these figures were analyzed after the war, a number of important military figures were led to the conclusion that chemical warfare had proved to be one of the most efficient and humane methods of waging war. In the context of this argument, a humane weapon is one that produces a low proportion of fatalities to casualties and of permanently disabled people to total casualties.

It is here that the apologists often make a glaringly illogical deduction: they go on to argue, by implication, that, because of this, all chemical and biological weapons are *more* humane than other weapons. They generalize, in other words, from figures taken from military action more than 50 years ago. Yet no biological weapons were used in World War I and so these figures can have no relevance to discussions of the humanity of biological agents. Secondly, the types of chemical in use then are for the most part now obsolete. They have been replaced primarily by the nerve gases, which, ironically enough, are likely to kill a far higher percentage of troops or civilians than most other weapons.

Of course, I have quoted the extreme form of this argument and it is only fair to redress the balance by quoting the U.S. Department of Defense. When in 1959 a resolution was put to the House of Representatives to reaffirm Roosevelt's "no first use" policy for chemical and biological weapons, the Department of Defense opposed the resolution with the following statement: "As research continues there is increasing evidence that some forms of these weapons, differing from previous forms, could effectively be used for defensive purposes with minimum collateral consequences."

This remark was referring to the development of incapacitating agents, such as the psychochemicals and the anaesthetic agents, which were thought capable of leading to "war without death." But it was made in 1959 and at the end of 1967 only one such agent had been standardized for use by the armed forces. This was BZ. Even that is now believed to have been "de-emphasized" in view of the unpredictability of its possible effects. So the arguments about humane chemical weapons refer mainly to a class of chemicals that have not yet been invented, with one exception which may never be used. Harassing agents —the tear gases and vomit gases—have also been included among the "humane" chemical weapons, and with a certain amount of reason. But these are relatively insignificant weapons, of more use in riot control than in any other type of action. They cannot be used either to support or to deny that chemical weapons in general are humane, and I shall return to this point at the end of this chapter.

What is true, however, is that some chemicals could be used to win battles with a minimum of permanent injuries and deaths. In this respect they are unique; they do, at least, offer the potentiality of producing injury-free war. But would they be used in that way? Is it any more moral or more humane to winkle an enemy out of a foxhole with tear gas and shoot him as he emerges than it is to throw a hand grenade down the foxhole in the first place? Yet this is the function of many of the harassing agents and the way in which they have been used in the past and probably will be used in the future. So far, chemicals are used only for their reversibly incapacitating effects in riot control, not war.

Most of the other arguments for using toxic weapons are not strictly concerned with moral issues but with practical ones. For instance, there is good evidence that the Soviet Union is in a high state of chemical preparedness, at least as far as defense is concerned. According to Theodor Rosebury, we simply do not know about the Soviet state of knowledge of biological weapons and there is little evidence that they have important research centers devoted to this subject. On the other hand, they probably would not talk about them if they did have them and so some strategists assume the Soviet Union possesses them. Strategists thus argue that there is little point in abandoning research in this field because other countries will continue with it: they see no sense in a unilateral policy of disarmament, if only because the Geneva Protocol preserves the right to retaliate in kind. This argument can be taken further to include the view that it would not be strategically wise to credit the Russians with the kind of moral scruples that might prevent them from using chemical and biological weapons. And if the Russians do not have these moral scruples, the argument runs, we cannot afford them either.

But there are other, more compelling practical arguments. The possession of chemical and biological weapons is said to give greater flexibility of wartime response. Without them, one is left with a simple choice between using conventional or nuclear weapons. Chemical and biological ones fill a gap and their existence means that there might be an occasion where we might eliminate the need to use nuclear devices.

Chemical and biological weapons are also very cheap, at least compared with nuclear weapons. Furthermore, they do not affect property and there may be many instances where it is essential to capture enemy territory without destroying its communication network, its roads, its factories, and its housing. The fact that these weapons do not deprive civilians of their possessions or homes can also be said to be humane. In Vietnam, for instance, the Vietcong have in some areas used civilians as shields. To capture the Vietcong would have required shooting both soldier and civilian. But the use of harmless and "reversible" tear gas enables the soldier to be captured (or shot) and the "shield" to be allowed to go free.

Lastly, it is argued, there are some jobs that cannot be done with anything but chemical weapons. In some places, for instance, the Vietcong underground tunnels are tens of miles long and destruction with explosives is only a temporary measure. The Vietcong return and dig the tunnels out again. If Vietcong are already in possession, it is difficult to capture the tunnels without loss of life. If they have left recently they usually boobytrap the underground complex. One solution has been to pump tear gas down the tunnels and drive the Vietcong out. This has worked up to a point but the gas can be pumped into the tunnel for only a fraction of its length; often it has simply driven the Vietcong deeper into his underground hideout. General Rothschild has recently argued that these tunnels could be cleared only with the help of mustard gas.

As this is persistent it would linger in the tunnel for months and penetrate throughout its ramifications. It would thus be made completely unoccupiable and notices warning of the mustard gas danger could be posted at every entrance to the complex to prevent anyone from being unnecessarily harmed. Again, this can be called a humane use of chemical agents.

Rothschild also argues that in the last world war there were many times when the Allies suffered heavy losses in close fighting to capture an island or town, but these losses could have been avoided if the occupied territory had first been attacked with chemicals and so made to surrender harmlessly. Fewer of the enemy, he argues, would also be killed that way.

Finally, there is the point that only chemical and biological weapons can be selected to produce either a lethal or an incapacitating effect. If you shell a town or bomb an airfield, the proportion of casualties to deaths is open to chance. If a man is hit by a bullet it is a matter of luck whether it kills or injures him. But with chemical and biological weapons, this can be decided in advance.

Clearly, some of these practical arguments are valid and chemical weapons, at least, are of great military use. But some of them can be countered with equally practical arguments. It is difficult to see, for instance, how the possession of toxic weapons by a nuclear power is likely to prevent that power being attacked with toxic weapons. A nuclear armory provides all the deterrent capability that could possibly be required. If toxic weapons are the only ones with which we can select a lethal or incapacitating effect in advance, biological weapons are also the only weapons that cannot be "aimed" (they propagate themselves). And if toxic weapons represent a more "flexible response," equally they represent to nonnuclear nations a cheap means of attaining the killing power of the nuclear stockpile.

And so it goes on. Perhaps the really important point about all these arguments is that they take off from very different viewpoints. They come into direct conflict only occasionally. It would seem, then, there is perhaps some hope of being able to resolve them. Points on both sides would have to be admitted as fact by the other side if they could be got together in a direct confrontation. But where the fundamental difference arises is over the time scale being considered. The arguments of the doves are based on long-term considerations, those of the hawks on short-term considerations. Overall, long-term views nearly always prove to be more valuable than short-term ones. For this reason, if for no other, it seems worth preserving our restraints on the use of chemical and biological weapons.

Biological warfare also raises quite separate moral issues about the status of the scientists and doctors who work on it. Hippocrates had much to say on the duties of doctors and by implication doctors of many nationalities have to agree to certain of these duties before gaining acceptance to their profession. Among the Hippocratic injunctions is the following: "I will use treatment to help the sick according to my ability and judgment, but never with a view to injury and wrong-doing. Neither will I administer a poison to somebody when asked to do so, nor will I suggest such a course . . ." The aim of today's current chemical warfare research has been aptly summarized as the search for "a cure for metabolism." It is clearly impossible to reconcile such a goal with the Hippocratic oath.

No nation can develop either chemical or biological weapons without aid from doctors. Whether doctors feel their consciences can remain clear if they work only on defensive projects is another matter. Dr. C. E. Gordon Smith, the Director of the Microbiological Research Establishment at Porton, has said he would lose many members of his staff if their work involved weapon development or offensive research. To work on the defensive measures associated with biological warfare might just have been approved by Hippocrates but he would surely have had graver doubts on the matter if he had stopped to consider how useful such defensive work might be for offensive preparations. He would certainly have wondered whether or not he might be able to advance the cause of medicine farther by taking a different job connected more directly with public health in peacetime.

Theodor Rosebury has written penetratingly about the ethical problems involved. In "Perspectives in Biology and Medicine" (Vol. 4, No. 4, University of Chicago) he said: "We resolved the ethical question just as other equally good men resolved the same question at Oak Ridge and Hanford and Chicago and Los Alamos. We were in a crisis that was expected to pass in a limited time, with a return to normal values. At Detrick a certain delicacy concentrated most of the physicians into principally or primarily defensive operations—*principally* or *primarily*: the modifiers are needed because military operations can never be exclusively defensive. The point is not extenuating. If extenuation is possible, and I think it is, it depends on the factor of time. We were fighting a fire, and it seemed necessary to risk getting dirty as well as burnt." Rosebury goes on to say that some argue that the crisis which persuaded doctors to take part in biological warfare research in the 1940s has never let up. What is their moral position now?

One of the important points, Rosebury believes, con-

cerns human experimentation and to what extent it con-
tradicts the Hippocratic injunction ". . . always to help,
never to hinder." Physicians have often reaffirmed the
principle that no experiments should ever be undertaken
on man if they involve any risk or any degree of coercion
—a phrase which is taken very seriously in the medical
profession and held to include not only bribes such as re-
mission of sentence for prisoners but also idealistic impulses such as those that might persuade a nurse or, presumably, a soldier to volunteer for experimentation. Yet
experiments connected with biological warfare have been
carried out. Humans have been exposed to aerosols of
Q-fever organisms in experiments in which every effort
was made to duplicate field conditions. The subjects were
"volunteers" but their exact status as volunteers was not
defined in the publications that described the results of
the experiments. Humans—some immunized and some
not—have also been experimentally exposed to plague and
as a consequence some of them contracted the disease.
Tests on volunteers have also shown that malaria and dengue fever can be deliberately transmitted by animal
vectors. Rosebury clearly regards these, and several other
instances in which the ethical problems connected with a
doctor's duty have been treated with a certain laxity, with
disrespect. He concludes: "I suggest that ethical principles
are not a luxury, that the essence of ethics—concern for
the value of man—is indispensable for the survival of
medicine as a profession, and doubtless also for the survival of mankind as a species."

One of the startling facts to emerge from a study of
the history of chemical warfare is the more or less complete reversal of attitude of the scientific community. In
the 19th century it was the scientists who suggested this
form of warfare and the generals who rejected it as being

virtually useless. During the First World War it was the scientists who got on with the job of developing new chemical weapons and providing defense against them. But it was the governments who inflamed public opinion against them and who were mainly responsible for fanning the emotional reactions against them which persist to this day. And after the war it was again the politicians who engineered the Geneva Convention of 1925, with the scientists playing only a background role. Indeed, some scientists at this time—including J. B. S. Haldane—wrote outspoken attacks on conventional weapons while praising the humane advantages which chemicals might offer.

But by the 1950s the roles were reversed. The scientific community, perhaps because of feelings of collective guilt for heralding in the age of nuclear weapons, began to protest in earnest. It seems that the scientific protests can almost be dated to the time when the nerve gases became a reality and when the chemical armory reached the same destructive capability as nuclear weapons themselves. In any event, the protests became louder, culminating in the mid-1960s with the resurgence of chemical warfare in Vietnam. Today that section of the scientific community that concerns itself with these issues at all is split down the middle, one half vigorously defending chemical and biological weapons, the other half attacking them with more fervor than has perhaps ever been applied by scientists to any political or military problem.

One of the first important protests was made in the spring of 1964 by the Federation of American Scientists —a body which since 1946 had concerned itself with the impact of science on national and world affairs. It called on the American President to declare a policy of "no first use" of both chemical and biological weapons and went on to request a cessation in the production of biological weapons and in the development of new chemical and biological weapons. The FAS view was that these weapons were likely to be used principally against civilians, which the FAS found to be "morally repugnant." They stressed the dangers of escalation, which might lead to a third world war. They pointed out that the advantage of developing such weapons was by no means clear as the United States already possessed a massive nuclear deterrent. What defensive measures were needed, they argued, involved rather broad problems of public health, which could easily be carried out in an open, nonsecret program. More significant, perhaps, was the FAS attitude to Vietnam where, at that time, the war was still on a relatively small scale.

The FAS said that officials had denied that anticrop agents were being used in Vietnam—although they did admit to the use of defoliation agents. But they went on to suggest that Vietnam was being used as a proving ground for chemical and biological warfare. They concluded: "We are further opposed to experimentation on foreign soil, and also feel that such experimentation involving citizens of other countries compounds the moral liability of such action." Whether or not Vietnam has ever been used as a proving ground for new chemical and biological weapons has never been satisfactorily resolved. But one thing is clear; the Americans have learnt much from their use of defoliation agents and anticrops chemicals in Vietnam. On the other hand, it is equally clear that chemicals have been used in Vietnam primarily for very real military purposes; if proving has been involved, it has been of secondary importance.

By September 1966 scientific reaction to the use of chemicals in Vietnam had greatly intensified. It was announced that a group of leading scientists had compiled a letter petitioning the President and warning him of the dangers of weakening restraints on the use of chemical and biological weapons. The hunt for signatures went on for some months until the letter was delivered at the White House on Valentine's Day, February 14, 1967. By that time 5,000 signatures had been collected and they included those of 22 Nobel Laureates and 127 members of the American National Academy of Sciences. This is, without doubt, the most important protest which has been penned to date and the letter is worth quoting in full:

Dear Mr. President,

We the American scientists whose names appear below wish to warn against any weakening of the world-wide prohibitions and restraints on the use of chemical and biological (CB) weapons.

CB weapons have the potential of inflicting, especially on civilians, enormous devastation and death which may be unpredictable in scope and intensity; they could become far cheaper and easier to produce than nuclear weapons, thereby placing great mass destructive power within reach of nations not now possessing it; they could lend themselves to use by leadership that may be desperate, irresponsible or unscrupulous. The barriers to the use of these weapons must not be allowed to break down.

During the second World War, the United States maintained a firm and clearly stated policy of not initiating the use of CB weapons. However, in the last few years the United States' position has become less clear. Since the late 1950's, the Defense Department expenditures on CB weapons have risen several fold—and there has been no categorical reaffirmation of the World War II policy.

Most recently, U.S. forces have begun the large-scale use of anti-crop and "non-lethal" anti-personnel weapons in Vietnam. We believe that this sets a dangerous precedent, with long-term hazards far outweighing any probable short-term military advantage. The employment of any one

CB weapon weakens the barriers to the use of others. No lasting distinction seems feasible between incapacitating and lethal weapons or between chemical and biological warfare. The great variety of possible agents forms a continuous spectrum from the temporarily incapacitating to the highly lethal. If the restraints on the use of one kind of CB weapon are broken down, the use of others will be encouraged.

Therefore, Mr. President, we urge that you:

Institute a White House study of overall government policy regarding CB weapons and the possibility of arms control measures, with a view to maintaining and reinforcing the world-wide restraints against CB warfare.

Order an end to the employment of anti-personnel and anti-crop chemical weapons in Vietnam.

Re-establish and categorically declare the intention of the United States to refrain from first initiating the use of chemical and biological weapons.

By the time the letter reached the White House it had been officially endorsed by both the Council of the Federation of American Scientists and by the Council of the Society for Social Responsibility in Science. But for all its pomp, for all its impressive list of signatures, the petition received no official acknowledgement. What reaction it did produce was from Pentagon sources, who asked not to be identified because the White House had not officially replied. According to *The New York Times* of September 21, 1966, these sources left no doubt that the Administration would continue using chemicals in Vietnam because they deemed it militarily useful. "What's the difference," a spokesman asked, "between denying the Vietcong rice by destroying it from the air or by sending in large numbers of ground forces to prevent the enemy from getting it? The end result's the same; only the first method takes less men." The other difference, which this spokesman omitted to mention, of course, is that with one technique the much needed food is destroyed and with the other it is eaten. If this is to be taken as the only official reaction, it was clear that the short-sighted policy was the one that was to be followed in Vietnam. Subsequent events proved this to be the case, for, although the use of antipersonnel weapons was reported less frequently, the defoliants and anticrop chemicals later began to be used on a far wider scale.

The petition did, however, serve at least one useful purpose: it sparked off intense public discussion of the issues involved. These raged for some months in the pages of scientific journals and it seemed that the discussion became progressively more sophisticated as time went on. Initially there was much confusion as to whether the protest was, in fact, a protest against the use of chemical weapons in particular or a protest against the Vietnam war—particularly unpopular with scientists—in general. It seems probable that the Administration interpreted it as the latter. Then, too, intelligent criticism was made of the petition itself on the grounds that it told the President to "review" policy and then proceeded to outline what the conclusions of this review should be. Petitioning scientists, it was felt, should be more scientific in their approach. The debate, as I have said, was slowly raised to a higher plane as some of those who had signed the petition saw that there were two points of view about the issues involved. Some scientists went so far as to claim that the antipersonnel chemicals used in Vietnam were humane in that they caused fewer deaths on both sides. Others asked whether or not the time really had come to try and make a clear cut distinction between chemical weapons, which were mainly controllable and predictable, and biological ones which were not. If for 50 years the two sides had been talking so loud neither could hear the voice of the other, they certainly got nearer together in 1967 than ever before. The extreme and preconceived viewpoints on each side became, for the first time, slightly eroded.

This activity was not due solely to this one petition. In September, 1966, 12 prominent plant physiologists sent another letter to the President, expressing their fear about the use of pesticides in Vietnam. They pointed out that chemicals designed to defoliate trees would be expected to have side effects on other plants, perhaps including crops. They were concerned, too, about how long the chemical might contaminate soil, preventing agriculture perhaps for some years into the future, and about the possible effects of these chemicals on humans and on domestic animals. They thought that the use of these chemicals might lead to grave ecological disturbances and that the use of chemicals against crops should properly be considered as a form of biological warfare, which was particularly invidious as the first victims of any resulting famine would be children, particularly those under five. The official reply, received 22 days later, read as follows:

Dear Mr. Galston,
    President Johnson has asked me to reply to your letter of September 6.
    Chemical herbicides are being used in Vietnam to clear jungle growth and to reduce the hazards of ambush by Vietcong forces. These chemicals are used extensively in most countries of both the Free World and the Communist Bloc for selective control of undesirable vegetation. They are not harmful to people, animals, soil or water.
    The elimination of leaves and brush in jungle areas enables our military forces, both on the ground and in the air, to spot the Vietcong and to follow their movements, and to also avoid ambushes.

Destruction of crops is undertaken only in remote and thinly populated areas under Vietcong control and where significant denial of food supplies can be effected by such destruction. This is done because in the Vietcong redoubt areas food is as important to the Vietcong as weapons. Civilians and non-combatants are warned of such action in advance. They are asked to leave the area and are provided food and good treatment by the Government of Vietnam in re-settlement areas.

Sincerely yours,
DIXON DONNELLEY
Assistant Secretary,
Department of Defense.

In one sense the reply seemed almost to confirm one of the fears of the petitioning scientists. It made no mention of whether or not the defoliating chemicals had a lasting effect and whether or not they were significantly harmful to other plants. This gave plant physiologists more cause to worry. Just how serious the threat to ecology in Vietnam is we shall probably not know for another five years. But the decision to turn the ten-mile wide demilitarized zone into a wasteland cannot have helped matters.

Further protests, both formal and informal, soon followed. Much the most important was made by the huge American Association for the Advancement of Science which has a membership of over 100,000 scientists. On December 30, 1966, their council passed the following resolution:

Whereas modern science and technology can now give man unprecedented power to alter his environment and affect the ecological balance of this planet; and

Whereas the full impact of the uses of biological and chemical agents to modify the environment, whether for peaceful or military purposes, is not known fully:

Be it resolved that the American Association for the Advancement of Science:

1. Expresses its concern regarding the long-range consequences of the use of biological and chemical agents which modify the environment; and

2. Establishes a committee to study such use, including the effects of chemical and biological warfare agents, and periodically to report its findings through appropriate channels of the Association; and

3. Volunteers its co-operation with public agencies and offices of government for the task of ascertaining scientifically and objectively the full implications of major programs and activities which modify the environment and affect the ecological balance on a large scale.

This resolution was again endorsed by the Society for Social Responsibility in Science.

Meanwhile, an issue which reached a far greater proportion of scientists had been receiving publicity at the University of Pennsylvania. Though many scientists take an active part in "advising" the government what uses they should or should not make of the results of scientific research, probably the majority have a more *laissez-faire* attitude. They would argue that the government is entitled to employ scientists to develop weapon systems if it chooses to and this is not of direct concern to a scientist working at a university or nongovernment research organization. The University of Pennsylvania affair shattered this complacency for many scientists when it was revealed that for some ten years scientists at this university had been working on chemical and biological warfare projects under government contract. Further, the scientists involved were not free to publish the results of their work and it was widely felt that this was a negation of all that academic research stood for.

The University had the government contract program well organized. They were conducted by a separate Institute for Co-operative Research on the university campus, which was headed by Dr. Knut A. Krieger—also Professor of Chemistry at the University—and comprised five other faculty members and eight graduate students. One project was known as Project Summit and was placed by the Defense Department for the preparation of information concerning offensive and defensive biological and chemical weapon systems. The other, an evaluation study of these weapons for the U.S. Air Force, was called Project Spice Rack. Together these projects were worth $845,000. The University brought pressure to bear on university officials who eventually announced that no further contracts would be undertaken unless the results could be freely published and that the Institute would be gradually phased out of relationship with the University. But no one would apparently commit themselves to not renewing the contracts if no other body could be found to take them on or if they appeared to be of even greater importance to national security. This left the body of the university totally unsatisfied and several members threatened to wear gas masks at university ceremonies unless the contracts were dropped.

At about this time, the split of opinion over the use of chemical and biological weapons was probed further by journals, which specialized in reporting major trends in science. A leader in *International Science and Technology,* for instance, found a lack of sympathy with the main petition to the President and claimed that we could no longer group chemical and biological weapons under the same head. Chemicals, it was argued, could be used humanely but the biological weapons probably could not and should be internationally banned. A more extreme view was taken by *Industrial Research,* an American magazine designed mainly for the scientist and technologist in industry, of whose readers more than ten percent fall into the industrial category of "ordnance." They dismissed most of the protests as emotional reaction against chemical and biological weapons and went on to argue that these weapons should be developed for they were potentially more humane than many conventional weapons. The arguments cited were strikingly similar to those used by General Rothschild in his book. But they did more than this. They held an opinion poll of what their readers thought of the use of chemical and biological weapons in general and in Vietnam in particular. The results, which were published in the February 1967 issue of the magazine, were as follows:

Do you feel that the United States is justified in employing CB weapons in Vietnam for . . .

   . . . crop destruction?
      Yes . . . 65 per cent   No . . . 35 per cent
   . . . defoliation of combat
      areas?
      Yes . . . 81 per cent   No . . . 19 per cent
   . . . nonlethal antipersonnel
      use?
      Yes . . . 79 per cent   No . . . 21 per cent
Do you think that lethal chemical or biological weapons should be used?
      Yes . . . 15 per cent   No . . . 65 per cent
     Only in certain cases . . . 20 per cent.
Should the United States continue to develop and test CB weapons even if they are not intended to be employed?
      Yes . . . 89 per cent   No . . . 11 per cent
Should the US make a firm declaration of restraint from the use of CB weapons at this time?

Yes . . . 33 per cent   No . . . 67 per cent

There has been considerable controversy concerning CB weapon development carried out at the University of Pennsylvania's Institute of Co-operative Research. Do you believe that military technology is inappropriate to a university?

Yes . . . 25 per cent   No . . . 60 per cent
Sometimes . . . 15 per cent

If this poll can be held reliable, it would seem that the consensus of opinion among industrial scientists is that chemical weapons at least should now be considered among the normal weapons of waging war. But, as we have seen, the opinion of many academic scientists is that all chemical and all biological weapons should be banned. Can this divergence of opinion be explained?

It seems that these two opinions concern two basically different aspects of the problem. Those who would have us use chemical weapons are concerned with the humanity of nonlethal chemical weapons in the short term. Those who would ban both types of weapon are concerned about the immense destructive power of lethal chemicals such as the nerve gases and the unknown results of large-scale biological attack. They are concerned with the long-term issues. In one sense there is something to be said for both views.

There is no doubt that the use of chemicals such as tear gases is relatively harmless, can save lives, and can be considered as humane. Doubtless other chemicals are now being developed that could also be classified as humane. If they could be used without any fear of further escalation into more dangerous chemicals or biological agents, many of those who have protested so vigorously about the use of chemicals in Vietnam might change their minds. But the issues are not really as simple as this and the consequences that have to be considered are of a much broader nature. The present agreement banning the use of chemical and biological agents is already hanging by a hair thread. International agreements about the use or prohibition of different weapon systems are perilously difficult to negotiate, as the nuclear weapon controversies have shown. Without being too pessimistic, it seems that the Geneva Protocol is fast on the way to becoming obsolete. The danger is that it will be scrapped before we have anything to take its place. If this happens, I cannot see anything that will prevent an all-out chemical and biological war in the future. Vietnam could turn out to be the Nagasaki of what Lord Ritchie-Calder has termed "the Doomsday Bug."

CHAPTER 11

The Scientist's Dilemma

> The scientists speak with an authority which the ordinary citizen, the non-scientist, cannot challenge, and to which he is compelled to listen. Since they cannot hope for much help from the generals or the ministers, they must act by themselves, in a supreme endeavour to avert the mortal dangers which confront mankind.
>
> P. Noel Baker.
> ("Science and Disarmament,"
> in *Impact,* vol. XV, no. 4, 1965)

WEAPONS have increased progressively in killing power throughout history. Each time they did so they caught the combatants, who found it difficult to readjust, by surprise; it was several months after the start of World War I, for instance, that officers gave up the habit of going into battle wearing swords. What is different about the current situation is that, in the past few years, we have learnt to look to the future with more apprehension and with more understanding. We know there will be further advances. We are not in the position of the eminent chemical commanders who, after World War I, peered murkily into the future to announce that there were no further chemical weapons to be invented—just 15 years before the Germans stumbled on the nerve gases.

This alone makes it unlikely that the future of weapons development will follow the same course as it has in the past. But there is another difference, which could turn out to be of even greater consequence. The world at large was first alerted to the threat of nuclear weapons after they had been developed—after they had been used, twice, in Japan. By this time the technological breakthrough had been made. The same is not now true of biological weapons. Of course, we can already visualize the potential danger they represent but the technological breakthrough required to make them into real military weapons is still some way ahead. In a sense this is encouraging. For although it took some 20 years to bring about a rather unsatisfactory control of nuclear weapons after the event, we have time on our hands, if we wish to control the use of biological weapons. About this we should not be complacent, for the time may be regrettably short. But already there are muffled political rumblings about the need to control biological weapons, and signs of important experimental action being taken by nonpolitical bodies such as Pugwash. There is a chance that in this field we could achieve a disarmament first; we could prevent the threat of a weapon before it is perfected.

It seems a slim chance—indeed it may be that we have already lost our chance. If this turns out to be the case, part of the blame must surely be layed at the feet of those who have been arguing so vehemently that in the toxic weapons we have our first chance to fight wars humanely. By using incapacitating chemical or biological agents, it has been suggested, we could make wars virtually harmless and nations might be persuaded to part with most of their other armaments—from machine guns to nuclear devices—and come to rely solely on "humane" chemical and biological weapons. Such an idea sounds more like a piece of wish fulfillment based on a misconception of what disarmament in the 20th century should really be about.

War does not exist in isolation. It is an instrument of national power, a weapon in the armory of foreign policy. Many now argue that it is an outdated weapon, an obsolete means of effecting national desires. As national importance declines as a military concept, and international trade, projects and cooperation grow as the basic components of the political machine, the need for war to resolve national conflict should diminish. In its place will come the weapons of future political cooperation—the sanctions produced by world trade, mutual education, and international cooperation. The beginnings of this change are already coming about; wars are now fought less often between individual nations than between political blocs. The chief hope of nearly all those involved in disarmament is not that we can devise ways to control the kinds of weapons that may be used in the future but that we can find alternatives to war as a means of resolving potential conflict.

There are brave new political concepts, which are strictly speaking outside the range of this book. But they are relevant in one important respect. If our aim is to eliminate war as a political weapon, the one thing we do not want is the development of a new series of weapon systems which make possible "benign war"—war in which no property is damaged and no one is irreversibly injured. It is only too easy to see how such weapons could become immensely popular—so much so that war might become an everyday activity. If so, it would surely bring about the destruction of all that is valued as human just as quickly as any nuclear war. The economic effects alone, and the atmosphere of political uncertainty that would ensue, could be enough to affect, this time perhaps irreversibly, the whole pattern of civilization. Weapons that rarely kill could turn out to be a very mixed blessing. Perversely, the fact that some of the more conventional ones do kill is a sanction against their use.

This is a powerful argument for not developing or using more incapacitating toxic weapons. Because the prospect of bringing about total world disarmament still seems extremely distant, one is left with an interim need to prevent all-out chemical or biological warfare. And this involves far more than making sure, or trying to make sure, that the remaining countries ratify the Geneva Protocol and that it is kept more closely in the future. This Protocol served an admirable purpose but one that may already be outdated. It is a Protocol that has been flouted in minor ways already and one which the United States have made it clear they are not bound by. Something else, both more fundamental and more enforceable, is needed.

The Geneva Protocol is concerned only with the use of toxic weapons in war. Is there any way in which disarmament or control could be effected at any earlier stage? One method of arms control, which has always been theoretically appealing, if practically remote, is to try and ensure that no country does research on a certain kind of weapon, does not test these weapons, and does not stockpile them. Clearly if a country is not developing a weapon and does not have it stockpiled we need no longer worry about international agreements banning its use in war. Could something along these lines improve the current situation?

The most fundamental means of attacking the problem would be to put a halt to all scientific research which might lead to improvements in chemical and biological weapons. This is clearly impossible. It would mean stopping nearly all important research in molecular biology, in public health, in pesticides, in organic chemistry, and in the study of all toxic substances. Almost every country in the world is carrying out some research along these lines and to halt it would be the most retrogressive step in science that has ever been made. Instead we must learn to live with scientific advance. As science progresses it throws out results, which may be put to good use—as in nuclear energy or the development of some pesticides. Equally, the same results may be put to bad use—as in the development of nuclear weapons and the nerve gases. To try and stop science because of this would be nonsense. Even to halt the kind of research that is going on in defense establishments such as those at Porton would be absurd because the scientific results leading to improved weapons are bound to come, if not from military establishments, then from university departments or hospitals.

But, it can be argued, if defense establishments were disbanded or the type of research carried out there was put on the "open market" of the university—where some claim it more properly belongs—we would at least be able to lessen international suspicion that every country is one step ahead of the next in the development of new toxic weapons. There is a great deal to be said for this argument. The trouble is that the kinds of research needed are so similar to what goes on anyway in open laboratories that we might be little better off. The suspicion would still lurk. The visiting team of inspectors, whose job it would be to make periodic inspections of research establishments, might still wonder if that vaccine production unit they visited last week—and which was then making vaccine—was still doing so. It would be so easy to convert it into apparatus for the manufacture of the raw material for biological warheads. The inspection problem would be almost impossibly difficult.

Secrecy has always been associated with chemical and biological warfare—much more so than in other fields of military technology. The research centers involved breed suspicion, sometimes quite unjustly, even though their security arrangements are not nearly so impressive nor their secrets so well kept as the details of the Chancellor's budget the day before he delivers his budget speech. Porton, for instance, is surrounded by only a low fence which could not possibly prevent the entry of anyone who seriously wanted to break in—and this fence, according to the Director of the M.R.E., is not to keep people out but to keep cows off the lawns! Yet the fact remains that Porton has a sinister image even though it is officially concerned only with defense and the M.R.E. there publishes about 80 percent of its work. The M.R.E. is an establishment that receives around 2,000 visitors a year and which, it is claimed, has relatively few secrets to hide. On the other hand, it does do work that is of major interest to other microbiologists and to public health officials. Channels of communication between civilian scientists and Porton do exist but they could doubtless be improved. If the unit were disbanded—and others like it in other parts of the world—would the world benefit more if the work were placed in open laboratories and the results made more freely available to other scientists? More important, would such a move serve any purpose in lessening international tension?

The answer to both questions must be yes. Very little of what goes on at the Microbiological Research Establishment at Porton would be out of place at a university or medical research center. And there can be no doubt that the existence of such a center does engender suspicion that more is going on there than perhaps really is. Why, then, does such a move not take place? This is not a novel idea and it has been mooted over a number of years. Indeed, the fact that it so far has not taken place has caused the resignation of a number of microbiologists from its staff. Some of the people who work there now do so because of its excellent equipment and the fact that it works on aspects of public health, for instance, which are not part of research programs elsewhere in the United Kingdom. The only drawback to this arrangement is the degree of security attached to their work and the possibility that what they are doing might one day be of direct relevance to a nation who wished to launch a biological attack.

But the move has not taken place. The units at Porton have not been disbanded and moved into open laboratories. Part of the reason is the extensive cooperation between Porton and its American equivalents. But a more important reason is simply that, however reluctant the Ministry of Defence says it would be to use biological weapons, the existence of Porton is reassuring. Officials know that in Porton are kept strains of virulent organisms, being tested for defense purposes, that could—if necessary—be turned into offensive weapons within a matter of days. Porton, and other units like it in France, Canada, and a host of other countries, are not as far as we know manufacturing biological weapons. But they could easily do so. For this very reason their existence does make the threat of biological warfare that much more real.

The dissolution of these establishments might therefore be helpful in controlling chemical and biological weapons. But it would be only marginally so and it would represent only a step in a chain of other actions which would have to follow. Even if these establishments were disbanded, there would be no guarantee that offensive work was not still proceeding under the protective arm of a university (as it apparently does in the United States) or a drug firm. Even the production of actual weapons could continue under this guise and if international agreements were to be reinforced by regular inspections the inspectors would have to look for two things: basic research into new weapons and the production of already developed ones. Both would be easy to conceal. Unlike the nuclear weapons—which require a huge industrial complex easily visible from the air for their manufacture—the biological ones need only a small building, hidden underground if necessary.

But since early 1964 Pugwash has been pinning some of its hopes on establishing just such an international inspection scheme. Pugwash has had committees studying the problems of chemical and biological warfare since the late 1950s but the first concrete steps were taken in 1964 at the 13th Pugwash conference on Science and World affairs, which was held at Karlovy Vary, in Czechoslovakia. A group was set up that found itself impressed by another scheme, which had recently been organized by members of the Western Europe Union. This was an agreement to submit to voluntary inspections for arms production, including chemical weapons. The idea that arose was that these countries, and others, might be persuaded to submit to similar inspection schemes for the production of biological weapons. A pilot scheme was run and biological research centers in four countries agreed to submit to inspection by a three-man team early in 1966. The institutes inspected were the Medical Research Council Group for Bacteriological Bioengineering in Stockholm, the State Serum Institute in Copenhagen, the Institute of Hygiene in Vienna, and the Institute of Microbiology in Prague. The exact form of the inspection was simplified by discussions with the International Atomic Energy Authority in Vienna, which is experienced in this field from its inspections of civilian nuclear centers. The results of this experiment were reported at the 16th Pugwash conference held in Sopot, Poland, in September 1966. Just before that, the Pugwash Study Group on Biological Warfare met in Stockholm. There they agreed that under the auspices of the Stockholm International Peace Research Institute they would elaborate plans for a control and inspection agency in such detail that they could be submitted for consideration by governments.

The four sites that were inspected were selected on the basis of their internationality—they represented countries on both sides of the Iron Curtain—and for their widely differing research fields. One was concerned with public health, one with general microbiology and one had facilities for the cultivation of a wide range of pathogens. One argument which suggests that such a scheme might at least approach technical feasibility is that biological warfare research could not be carried out in any microbiological laboratory. Two of the essential requirements, for instance, would be a large supply of experimental laboratory animals and mass production apparatus for the cultivation of bacteria or viruses. Even so, the number of potentially dangerous laboratories is enormous in a country with as much scientific research going on as the United Kingdom or France. Where the scheme might prove more useful, perhaps, is among the smaller countries, particularly in Europe, which are not already committed to research programs in biological warfare for either defense or offense. It seems very doubtful whether the governments of the United States and the Soviet Union could ever be convinced of the efficacy of such an inspection scheme. And, if they were, they would certainly have to undergo a radical change of heart before they would agree to it. At the moment they have too much to hide and, in the States at any rate, an inspection team would know exactly where to go to find just what it was looking for. The inspection would be really useful only after major countries had agreed the need to abandon offensive research and development programs. This is a very long-term proposition and Pugwash has wisely been keeping its eyes on other ways of easing international tension.

At the risk of repetition, I should perhaps clarify the issues involved in biological disarmament. Ideally one would like to bring about an agreement to halt research in these areas—that is, military research designed specifically to provide new knowledge about these weapons and their possible lines of development. This could be achieved only if backed by an inspection system of the type I have been describing. Failing that, one could aim at an agreement not to test such weapons. Or, and this is the least satisfactory arrangement and the one which is now in partial operation, one can make an international agreement not to use such weapons in war. Let us deal with these last two points in turn.

We are still in the midst of negotiations not to test nuclear weapons. So far, of course, limited success has been achieved in that agreements have been reached that nuclear weapons will be tested only underground. This has served a very useful purpose and has effectively put an end to the mounting levels of radioactivity which were being found in the atmosphere as a result of atmospheric tests. At the present time, only China is engaged in atmospheric testing. And there is reasonable hope that eventually a total test ban treaty will be reached which will forbid the testing of nuclear weapons even underground. But there are technical difficulties here. The most important is that it is difficult to detect underground nuclear explosions from a distance, particularly if the explosions are small ones. It is also difficult to distinguish such tests from small seismic disturbances. This has meant that, in spite of the network of underground detection systems that is installed all over the world, one nation could still not be absolutely certain that another has not carried out small and isolated underground nuclear tests. But it could be certain if it were allowed to make a few spot checks in "enemy" territory every year. So far, the present atmosphere of mutual distrust has prevented such an arrangement from being set up, although it is well within the bounds of technical feasibility. The total test ban treaty, therefore, was first delayed by a lack of certainty about detection systems and, now that these technical problems have been virtually overcome, by a new series of political difficulties. Pugwash argue that, if a biological detection system could be produced, we might be able to negotiate an international agreement not to test such weapons even without requiring spot checks to be made on suspected biological centers. This would be at least a step forward from a partially kept treaty that prevents such weapons only from being used in war. It interrupts the military chain, as it were, at an earlier stage because, before a weapon is used, it will have to be tested.

Unfortunately, a biological detection unit poses grave technical problems. The idea is that to test a biological weapon satisfactorily will involve detonating the weapon, releasing the biological material over a wide area on a proving ground—such as the American one in Dugway, Utah—and recording the results on experimental animals set up in the area. There is a chance that, because an aerosol will have to be used, stray particles with biological activity could be detected at some distance from the testing center. It seems to me that if this is true, the testing is likely to constitute a threat to civilian populations in any case —and would probably act in this way as its own detection system. But it is also true that the incidence of even half a dozen cases of a quite rare disease in a civilian population could not be taken as strict proof of a biological test. It is always possible the disease could have arrived naturally. Any detection system, then, would have to distinguish between natural particles and particles from a biological test. How this could be done is not yet known in any detail and it seems to be some way from a technical solution. The current situation is that a Pugwash study group has been set up to investigate the technicalities of such a system and to report at the earliest opportunity.

Though difficult, this is a project well worth pursuing. If highly successful, it might even form the basis for a total biological test ban treaty of the kind I mentioned earlier. But even if the resulting system was of only limited efficiency, it might provide a number of technical by-products in the arms control field. For instance, if some nations could be persuaded to maintain such detection devices, this would at least provide some reassurance that these nations were not themselves participating in biological tests. Equally, it would show other nations that the participating ones were seriously concerned about the problem. And the possibility—however small—that a biological test might be detected could well deter a state from conducting a large-scale test of a biological weapon, even in the absence of a test ban treaty.

Pugwash is also working on a rapid detection system designed to provide immediate warning of a biological attack and identification of the particular kind of biological agent being used. This is a somewhat simpler problem for the system would need to be far less sensitive and it is one that is already being attacked by several military establishments throughout the world for defense purposes. The technical details of such a system have already been discussed in Chapter 9 and I will not repeat them here. The Stockholm International Peace Research Institute has, however, agreed to cooperate with Pugwash in a research program to develop such a system, preferably in conjunction with stations such as the Microbiological Research Establishment at Porton. This is an important project and one which could find major applications in public health—for identifying the entry of smallpox virus into a country, for instance—and for defense.

Another application of a detection system of this kind might be to establish the truth about cases where one side accuses the other of using biological warfare. What is needed here, perhaps more than a detection system, is an international agency with the power to investigate allegations about the use of biological warfare. The most serious allegation of this kind to occur so far was the one that took place in Korea and China in 1952. As I have said, the committee called in to investigate found the case proven but not to the satisfaction of the majority of nations. This was an incident that did a lot to worsen already bad relationships between the two sides. One can easily envisage other occasions on which an allegation of this kind might be made simply to heighten international tension. If a body were established to investigate these accusations to everybody's satisfaction, one weapon in international intrigue could be eliminated.

I have dealt in some detail with what may seem to be only minor efforts to establish biological disarmament because these are the only efforts currently being made. It is lamentable that there is at the moment no governmental action of any kind being made to control chemical and biological weapons, or to slow down their speed of development. This is in spite of the fact that our main existing constraint—the Geneva Protocol—has been recently, seriously and perhaps finally violated by the Americans in Vietnam. This current inactivity compares extremely ill with the range and farsightedness of the first efforts that were made as long ago as the 17th century.

The first international agreement about toxic weapons was probably the Treaty of Strasburg of 1675 in which poisoned bullets were outlawed. In 1874 the Brussels conference included recommendations for outlawing the use of poison or poisoned weapons but they were never ratified. But 25 years later, in 1899, the Hague Peace Conference met at The Hague and the first attempt to prohibit gas warfare was made. It was then the first American objections to this kind of treaty made themselves felt and the United States did not sign the declaration, saying in effect that all weapons were barbarous and that if effective gas weapons were invented (they were not at that time in existence) they would probably be used, regardless of any agreement reached, under the stress of war. The situation with regard to chemical warfare in 1899 has too many similarities with the present situation as regards biological warfare for any of us to extract any comfort from it. In 1899 there was an international agreement to which all major nations subscribed, with the exception of the United States, and which banned the use of chemical weapons which at that time had not been perfected. Yet within 16 years chemical weapons were to be used in a world war on a massive scale by many of the nations who had signed the agreement. Today we have an international agreement that includes a ban on the use of bacteriological weapons which all the major nations have ratified with the exception of the United States. Again, the agreement is to prohibit the use of a weapon—this time a biological one—which has not yet been perfected. If history really does repeat itself, the future does not look bright.

After the First World War a number of efforts were made to prevent the recurrence of the chemical nightmare still in everyone's mind. Treaties were signed in Versailles in 1919 and also in Neuilly-sur-Seine. In 1921-22 a conference in Washington between the United States, France, Italy, the British Empire, and Japan agreed not to use asphyxiating or poisonous substances and analogous materials in war. This was ratified by all the participants with the exception of France, who objected on the grounds of a quite different clause concerning the uses of submarines. Consequently the treaty never came into force, although it is the only one that received the approval of the United States Senate.

In 1925, of course, came the Geneva Protocol, the first agreement to include specific mention of bacteriological as well as chemical warfare. At the time 29 nations signed the treaty and many more have now ratified it. The United States, Japan, Brazil, and Uruguay have not ratified it and neither have a number of much smaller countries. But there is a reasonable hope that many of these countries may do so in the future. The Geneva Protocol of 1925 was considered at a General Assembly of the United Nations held in December 1966. A motion was put forward that, in effect, called on all member nations strictly to observe the Protocol and invited them to accede to it. The motion was passed, with 91 nations voting for it, none against it, and only four abstaining. Both the United States and Japan voted for the resolution and so, in effect, made public their intention to abide by the Protocol.

How can such an action be reconciled with American use of chemical agents in Vietnam? There are two possible explanations. The first is that a vote in favor of a motion at the U.N. General Assembly does not necessarily mean that the policy of the country concerned will explicitly follow that motion. Before that can happen, the motion must be accepted also by parliamentary procedures within the country. We should remember that the United States signed the Geneva Protocol of 1925 but subsequently the American Senate rejected the agreement and it was consequently never ratified by the United States. It is likely that the Senate will exercise their blocking power yet again if called upon to follow up the U.N. motion of 1966.

The second explanation is concerned with the shortcomings of the wording of the Geneva Protocol. Specifically, this prohibits the use in war of asphyxiating, poisonous, or other gases and of bacteriological methods of warfare. International lawyers who have examined the Protocol in detail find reason to believe that it refers only to the use of these agents against man and not to their use against crops or against animals. So technically the use of defoliants and herbicides is not an infringement of the Protocol. American officials have also argued that the Protocol refers specifically to the use of these agents in war and that technically the United States has not declared war on any nation in Vietnam. Therefore, it might be claimed, the Protocol would not apply to any of their actions in that country, even if the United States had ratified the Protocol. And lastly, it has also been argued that the antipersonnel chemicals used in Vietnam are not technically asphyxiating or poisonous.

To most people the arguments quoted above would suggest not that the American action in Vietnam is morally justified but only that there is a legal loophole through which the United States might have been able to wriggle if she had ratified the Protocol. This means that international law does need tightening up. The intent of the Geneva Protocol should be made to apply strictly to situations that, while not technically constituting war, are indistinguishable from it in practice. It should not be beyond international lawyers, for instance, to find a wording that specifically forbids the use of chemical and biological warfare in Vietnamese-like situations yet still permits tear gases to be used for riot control (where, as I have said, there is no risk of chemical escalation). Secondly, it might also be advisable to extend the Geneva Protocol to forbid the use of chemical and biological agents against crops and animals. But there are technical problems involved here and the situation is so complicated that it would not be profitable to discuss it at greater length.

After the Second World War a General Assembly of the United Nations sought to eliminate weapons of mass destruction which were to include lethal chemical and biological weapons. No mention was made of incapacitating chemical or biological weapons. Subsequently there have been numerous small agreements between European nations. Italy and Germany, for instance, have agreed not to undertake the manufacture of chemical or biological weapons on their territory and Austria has agreed not to possess, construct, or experiment with them.

Where does this leave us today? The situation is perilous. Vast sums of money are being spent on weapons which may prove as devastating in their effects as anything so far invented and which may turn out to be within financial reach of any country wishing to use them. The prospects for international control by inspection schemes and detection apparatus are remote. The only major international treaty forbidding the use of these weapons in war has not been ratified by the country whose expenditure in the field is greater than any, and which is violating the intent of that treaty on an increasingly massive scale. The chances of getting the major powers to agree to signing a new treaty prohibiting the use of these weapons is small. If they did, the chances that the treaty would be adhered to are equally small. History has shown us that we agree to such conditions only when we want to. It is essentially a practical problem and not one that can be solved by any degree of wish fulfillment that the human race will suddenly see the folly of its ways and abandon its efforts in this particular field of military enterprise. If that was possible before the invention of the nuclear weapon, it is certainly not even feasible after it. Nations have learned that their military future is inextricably entwined with scientific advance. They will not release their grasp on science easily.

If there is a ray of hope—and admittedly it seems an obscure one—it is in the fact that the next era of warfare could not take place without the cooperation of scientists. Although scientists have accustomed themselves to a military role they are for the most part, I believe, reluctant to take part in any experimentation that might pave the way to more sophisticated chemical and biological weapons. In a sense they have learned their lesson at Los Alamos, at Bikini, at Hiroshima, and at Nagasaki. In the event it proved far more difficult to enlist the help of highly trained scientists to develop the postwar hydrogen bomb than it did to enlist scientific aid in developing the atomic bomb during the war.

This is not the place to probe into the question of scientific responsibility for ushering in the nuclear age. The consensus of opinion is that it was politicians who misused the power that scientists provided them with. To my mind this is a facile argument. A portion of the blame must surely belong to those scientists—on all sides—

who helped foster the idea that an atomic weapon might be feasible and that the other side might be producing it. Once this was established there was no alternative but to develop the weapon as a means of defense which, as it turned out, was to be first used by the Allies in offense.

In the field of chemical and biological weapons, the scientific community has its first real opportunity to make amends. By denying their support to any defensive or offensive work on either kind of weapon system, they could effectively remove the threat of massive chemical or biological war in the future. They could do it quickly. They could do it tomorrow. They could do it finally. For let there be no mistake about this. No government can develop further weapons in this field without the help of scientists. A denial of their willingness to cooperate would put an end to chemical and biological escalation and there would be nothing that any democratically elected government could do about it.

This is the scientist's dilemma. But because of human nature, I fear they will not grasp the opportunities for peace that are within their reach. But let us at least remember that in the relatively peaceful late 1960s the scientific community held the decision in the palm of its hand. If they choose to usher in the realm of biological warfare they must, this time, take the responsibility for it. They cannot plead that their survival is threatened if they do not cooperate.

Bibliography

"Agriculture's Defense Against Biological Warfare and Other Outbreaks," *Agricultural Research Service Special Report,* United States Department of Agriculture, December 1961.

Bc-stridsmedel (in Swedish), *FOA orienterar OM,* 2 (December 1964).

Beller, William S., "Fireflies to Light the Way in N.A.S.A. Effort to Chart Earth's Biosphere," *Missiles and Rockets,* Vol. 16, No. 10 (March 8, 1965).

"Biological and Chemical Warfare, An International Symposium," *Bulletin of the Atomic Scientists,* XVI (June 1960).

Bowmer, Ernest J., "Preparation and Assay of the International Standards for *Clostridium botulinum* Types A, B, C, D and E Antitoxins," *Bulletin of the World Health Organization,* Vol. 29 (1963), pp. 701-709.

Brooksby, J. B., "Foot-and-mouth Disease—a World Problem," *Nature* (January 14, 1967).

Carlat, Louis E., "Germs and Gases," *Nuclear Information,* Vol. V., No. 4 (February 1963).

"Chemical and Biological Warfare," *Scientist and Citizen,* Vol. 9, No. 7 (August–September 1967).

"Civil Defense against CBR, ACS Gives Warning at CBR Defense and ACS News," *Chemical and Engineering News,* 37, (1959), p. 42.

Clarke, Robin, "Biological Warfare," *Science Journal,* Vol. 2, No. 11 (November 1966).

Crozier, Dan, "Survival in Germ Warfare," *Ordnance* 49, (1965), p. 530.

Crozier, Dan, Tiggert, William D., and Cooch, Joseph W., "The Physician's Role in the Defense Against Biological Weapons," *J.A.M.A.,* Vol. 175, No. 1 (January 7, 1961).

Dewsbery, J. P., "Schizophrenia and the Psychotomimetic Drugs," *Endeavour,* Vol. 19, No. 73 (January 1960).

"FAS Statement on Biological and Chemical Warfare," *Bulletin of the Atomic Scientists,* (October 1964).

FM 27-10 "The Law of Land Warfare," Department of the Army, Washington, D.C., *Government Printing Office,* (July 1956).

Fothergill, LeRoy D., "Biological Agents in Warfare and Defence," *New Scientist,* (November 30, 1961).

Gordon Smith, C. E., "The Microbiological Research Establishment, Porton," in *Chemistry and Industry,* No. 69 Research Establishments in Europe (1967), p. 336.

Granzeier, Frank J., "Toxic Weapons," *Industrial Research,* (August 1965).

Green, H. L., and Lane, W. R., "Particulate Clouds," 2nd ed., Spons., (London 1964).

Harper, G. J., "The Influence of Environment on the Survival of Airborne Virus Particles in the Laboratory," *Archit fur die Gestamte Virusforschung,* XIII (1963), pp. 1-3.

Hawkes, Russel, "Nose May Sniff out Systems Problems," *Missiles and Rockets,* (February 1, 1965).

Heden, Carl-Goran, "Defences against Biological Warfare," in press *Ann. Rev. Microbiol.* (1967).

Hollyhock, W. M., "Weapons Against the Mind," *New Scientist,* (April 22, 1965).

Holmstedt, B., "Pharmacology of Organophosphorous Cholinesterase Inhibitors," *Pharmacol. Revs.,* 11 (1959), pp. 567-688.

Hood, A. M., "Infectivity of Influenza Virus Aerosols," *Journal of Hygiene,* 61 (Camb. 1963), p. 331.

Hood, A. M., "Infectivity of *Pasteurella tularensis* clouds," *Journal of Hygiene* 59 (Camb. 1961), p. 497.

Humphrey, J. H., "Initiative Against Chemical and Biological

Warfare," *New Scientist,* (29 September 1966).

Langer, Elinor, "Chemical and Biological Warfare I and II," *Science,* Vol. 155 (13 January 1967), pp. 174-79 and (20 January 1967), pp. 299-303.

Langer, William L., "The Black Death," *Scientific American* (February 1964).

Liebermann, E. J., "Psychochemicals as Weapons," *Bulletin of the Atomic Scientists,* 18 (1962), pp. 11-14.

Lindsey, D., "Selective Malfunctioning of the Human Machine," *Military Med.,* 125 (1960), pp. 598-605.

MacArthur, D. M., "CBN Defense," *Ordnance* 9-10 (September-October 1965), p. 133.

"Materials on the trial of former servicemen of the Japanese Army charged with manufacturing and employing bacteriological weapons," Foreign Languages Publishing House, (Moscow, 1950).

"Nonmilitary Defense, Chemical and Biological Defenses in Perspective," *Advances in Chemistry Series No. 26,* Washington, D.C., American Chemical Society (1960).

Nopar, R. E., "Plagues on Our Children," *Clinical Pediatrics,* Vol. 6, No. 2 (February 1967).

Postgate, J. R. and Hunter, J. R., "Metabolic Injury in Frozen Bacteria," *Journal of Applied Bacteriology,* Vol. 26, No. 3 (December 1963).

Postgate, J. R. and Hunter, J. R., "The Survival of Starved Bacteria," *Journal of Applied Bacteriology,* Vol. 26, No. 3 (December 1963).

"Proceedings of Pugwash Conference of International Scientists on Biological and Chemical Warfare," Pugwash, Nova Scotia, Canada (August 24-30, 1959).

"Pugwash Study Group on Biological Warfare," *Pugwash Newsletter,* Vol. 4, Nos. 1 and 2 (July-October 1966), p. 29.

"Report of the International Scientific Commission for the Investigation of the facts concerning bacterial warfare in Korea and China" (Peking, 1952).

Rinkel, Max, Atwell, Charles R., DiMascio, Albert, and Brown,

Jonathan, "Experimental Psychiatry. V-Psilocybine, a New Psychotogenic Drug," *The New England Journal of Medicine,* Vol. 262, No. 6, (February 11, 1960), pp. 295-297.

Robinson, Julian Perry, "Chemical Warfare," *Science Journal,* Vol. 3, No. 4 (April 1967).

Rosebury, Theodor, "Medical Ethics and Biological Warfare," *Perspectives in Biology and Medicine,* VI (1963), p. 4.

Rosebury, Theodor, *Peace or Pestilence,* McGraw-Hill, (1949).

Rothschild, J. H., "Germs and Gas; The Weapons Nobody Dares Talk About," *Harper's Magazine,* Vol. 218, No. 1309 (June 1959), p. 29.

Rothschild, J. H., "Propaganda and Toxic War," *Ordnance,* 50 (1966), pp. 617-619.

Rothschild, J. H., *Tomorrow's Weapons,* McGraw-Hill (1964).

Sartori, M., *The War Gases* (London 1943).

Saunders, B. C., "Toxic Phosphorus and Fluorine Compounds," *Endeavour,* Vol. 19, No. 73 (January 1960).

Schneir, Walter, "The Campaign to Make Chemical Warfare Respectable," *The Reporter,* Vol. 21, No. 5 (October 1st 1959), p. 24.

Shewan, J. M., and Cann, D. C., "Botulism and Fishery Products," Torry Advisory Note No. 22, Ministry of Technology, Torry Research Station, H. M. Stationery Office (May 1965).

Sidel, V. W., and Goldwyn, R. M., "Chemical and Biological Weapons—a Primer," *New England Journal of Medicine,* 274 (January 6, 1966), pp. 21-27 and 50-51.

Strange, R. E., and Ness, A. C., "Effect of Chilling on Bacteria in Aqueous Suspension," *Nature,* Vol. 197, No. 4869 (February 23, 1963), p. 819.

U.S. House of Representatives, Committee on Foreign Relations, "Chemical—Biological—Radiological (CBR) Warfare and its Disarmament Aspects," (86th Cong., 2nd Sess., Committee Print), Washington, D.C., Government Printing Office, (1956).

U.S. House of Representatives, Committee on Science and Astronautics. "Chemical, Biological and Radiological Warfare Agents," (86th Cong., 1st Sess., Hearings), Washington, D.C., Government Printing Office (1961).

Wachtel, Curt, "Chemical Warfare," Chemical Publications Co., Inc. (1941).

Wood, J. R., "Chemical Defense," *Journal of the American Medical Association,* 145 (1951), pp. 1264-1267.

Index

Index

263

Biological warfare (*Continued*)
popular misconception about, 100
U.S. expenditures on, 7, 19, 32-33

Biological weapons
agriculture and, 1-2
development, 1-11

Black Death, 67, 77, 78
casualties, 64, 66
origin of, 66

Black rats, 65, 68

Black stem rust, 142-143

Blood gases, 189

Boccaccio, Giovanni, 67

Boer War, 16

Botulinum toxin, 89, 91-92, 96, 120, 202
stockpiling, 108-109

Botulism, 89-90

Bourlon Wood, battle at, 38

Breakbone fever, 110-111

Brooklyn College, 9

Brucella abortus, 75

Brucella melitensis, 102

Brucella suis, 124

Brucellosis, 75, 96, 102, 115, 152-153
producing, 93
symptoms of, 153

Brussels conference of 1874, 237

Buboes, defined, 66

Bubonic plague, 65-66, 68

Bulletin of the Atomic Scientists, 26-30, 200

BZ (hallucinogenic drug), 55-56, 58

Cacodylic acid, 15, 145

Cactoblastis, 155

Carlat, Louis E., 116

Carson, Rachel, 3

Catlin, G., 79

Chemical Defence Experimental Establishment (Great Britain), 50-51, 192

Chemical warfare
agriculture and, 1-2

arguments against, 197-223; civilian population and, 197-199; international, 199, 201, 206, 223; medical profession and, 209-210; scientists, 209-223

beginning of, 12

crop destruction, 136-147

defense preparations, 172-196; advance warning and, 174-177; experimental devices in, 178-180; fallout shelters, 186-187; gas mask, 173, 184-186, 188; identifying chemicals and, 177; research programs, 178-180

disarmament and, 224-242; international inspection, 231-234, 240; research secrecy, 229; scientific responsibility, 241-242

livestock destruction, 136, 147-154

military role, 158-171; compared to nuclear weapons, 159-161, 164-165; in guerrilla warfare, 165-168; limitations, 161-164; sabotage, 169-171

protection against, 104

research programs, 7-9, 53, 56-59

U.S. expenditures on, 7, 19, 32-33

Vietnam War, 136-137, 139-140, 145-147; Geneva Protocol and, 238-240; scientists' reaction to, 213-223

weapon development, 1-11

World War I, 3, 4, 15-18, 34-41, 45; effects of, 106; kinds of, 39

World War II, 41-46; Germany and, 44-46, 49

Chinese Peace Committee, 22

Chlorine gas, 35-37

Chloromycetin, 114

Cholera, 18, 21, 70-75, 118
as biological agent, 114
causes of, 73

Streptomycin, 71, 94
Stubbs, Marshall, 132, 158
Suez Canal, 81
Sulphur dioxide, 16
Sunday Mainichi, 23-24
Synthetic insecticides, 13
Syphilis, 95

Tabun, 41, 44, 46, 48
  toxicity, 42
  U.S.S.R. stockpile, 49-50
Tear gases, 34, 49, 202, 205
  detecting, 174
  in riot control, 202-203
  in Vietnam War, 166
Theiler, Max, 83, 97-98
Thucydides, 67
Tomorrow's Weapons (Rothschild), 44, 204
Toxins
  defined, 89
  types of, 89-90
Trachoma, 112
Tuberculosis, 70, 106
Tularemia, 92-93, 94, 104, 118
  as biological agent, 114
2,4,5,-Trichlorophenoxyacetic acid, 145
Typhoid, 21
Typhus, 18-19, 113

Undulant fever, 152-153
United Nations, 238, 239
United Nations Genocide Convention of 1948, 199
United States Agricultural Research Service, 143-144
United States Army
  Chemical Warfare laboratories, 58
  Field Manual FM 3-10, 47
  Field Manual FM 27-10, 10
  Guided Missile Department, 47-48
United States Chemical Corps, 116
United States Department of Defense, 7, 10, 48, 166, 205
United States Department of State, 10

United States Public Health Service, 9, 60
University of Chicago, 9
University of Maryland, 9
University of Michigan, 9
University of Minnesota, 9
University of Pennsylvania, 9, 219-220
University of Texas, 9
University of Utah, 9

V agents, 46-47
  toxicity, 47
Venezuelan equine encephalomyelitis, 124, 182-183
Versailles Treaty, 238
Vibrio comma, 73
Vicksburg, battle at, 15
Vietnam War, 1, 7, 24, 49, 85, 237
  chemical warfare, 33, 136-137, 139-140, 145-147, 165-168; Geneva Protocol and, 238-240; scientists' reaction to, 213-223
  civilian casualties, 198
  crop destruction in, 131, 136-137, 139-140, 145-147
  defoliation operations, 131, 145-147, 166
  gases used in, 60-61, 62-63, 166
  guerrilla warfare in, 165-168
  melioidosis in, 72
  plague in, 68-69
Virulence, defined, 92
Viruses, 76-83, 91-92, 106
  ability to transfer genetic material, 99-100
  antianimal for biological agents, 150
  breeding attenuated strains of, 97
  drawback as biological weapons, 109-112
  forming of, 76
  intestine infecting, 110
  respiratory, 110
  techniques for growing, 95
  transmitted by animal vectors, 110-111